THE ROTHKO CHAPEL

An Act of Faith

THE ROTHKO CHAPEL

An Act of Faith

Susan J. Barnes

A ROTHKO CHAPEL BOOK

Distributed by University of Texas Press · Austin

1 9 8 9

Cover: Mark Rothko in his 69th St. studio with chapel paintings in progress, New York, 1965, photograph by Alexander Liberman

Back cover: Albrecht Dürer, woodcut (detail, simplified reproduction), 1505, after a drawing by Leonardo da Vinci

Frontispiece: Rothko Chapel (exterior), 1988, with Barnett Newman's *Broken Obelisk*

Library of Congress Cataloging-in-Publication Data

Barnes, Susan J.

The Rothko Chapel. An Act of Faith.

Bibliography: p.

   1. Art, American–Texas–Houston
   2. Art, Modern–20th century–Texas–Houston
   3. Rothko Chapel (Houston, Texas)
   4. Houston, (Tex.)–Buildings, structures, etc.
   I. Menil, John de
  II. Menil, Dominique de
 III. Rothko, Mark
 IV. Newman, Barnett
  V. Johnson, Philip
 VI. Title

N6535.H68B37 1987   726'.5'097641411   87-28257

ISBN 0-945472-00-5

Distributed by
University of Texas Press
P.O. Box 7819; Austin, Texas 78713-7819

Printed in the United States of America

Contents

*"Ici
devraient
venir
les enfants
du monde entier
à qui on dirait
Voilà…"* *

[*Here, the children of the whole world
should come, and be told: "This is it …"*]

* Comments from visitors to
the Rothko Chapel

Preface

"A Stonehenge for us" *

Among the great artistic achievements of the mid-twentieth century, the Matisse Chapel in Vence and the Rothko Chapel in Houston stand out as master works of religious art. Henri Matisse, though he had not been religiously inclined, devoted four years of his life to a chapel for Dominican sisters. He said that it was "the crowning of his career." Fifteen years later, Rothko, also without religious convictions, created an ecumenical chapel in Houston which he considered his greatest achievement.

That such jewels were made for spiritual quest and celebration in a time of general unbelief among artists and intellectuals reminds us, once more, that real creators, always working at the limit of their perceptions, may reach spiritual regions bordering on the sacred.

Rothko succeeded in translating his passionate quest into sublime art. Inhabited by the tragedy of the human condition, he attempted to express its poignancy. "Somewhere in him was the lover of the absolute," wrote Dore Ashton.

As a marvelous fruit of his sensitivity and his travail, through agonizing hours of doubt and searching, Rothko created a modulated ensemble of majestic paintings. The dark purplish tones have a soothing effect, yet they retain enough brilliance to stimulate the mind. The black surfaces invite the gaze to go beyond. The chapel is a place conducive to spiritual activity. We are cut off from the world and its suffocating multiplicity, able to wander in the infinite. Lacking the immensity of the desert, it is in the confines of a restricted place that we can best embrace "the whole." Here we are nowhere and everywhere; here we can find a blessed wholeness, a sense of unity.

Visitors have commented on their impressions. Some have been disconcerted, even frankly hostile. It is not easy to absorb such an uncommon place as the Rothko Chapel. The space has a destabilizing effect on established views and modes of thinking. The mood of the remarks shifts from rejection to perplexity, to awe, to peace:

> "Being in the chapel is an emotional experience in which you either face your innermost self or leave in incomprehension, possibly even fear."

> "The feeling of tranquility and majesty is astounding."

Remarks on peace abound. There is also an awakening to higher realities, responding to the challenge of the paintings:

> "In hope we can all reach that point in us that is everything."

> "A place not to think — to unthink."

> "There is no there, – here."

People come from all over the world and from every persuasion. "We traveled 2000 miles to see it. It's certainly worth it." A Londoner noted: "I came to Houston especially to experience this. I am richer and wiser . . . and grateful." A Yugoslavian couple wrote: "It gave us strength and spiritual peace. It is beautiful and uplifting." And:

> "seldom have I felt more in the presence of God."

> "mind and space before God."

Time and again the word *God* appears. We are in an Anglo-Saxon country where the source of all life, the One without a name, with an infinity of names, whispered, breathed . . . El. . . Al . . . Elohim . . . Allah, the One compared to light and proclaimed Zeus, Theos, Dios, . . . is called God—a sound that has a dullness which struck Lawrence of Arabia who wrote: "We lost much eloquence when making Him the shortest and ugliest of our monosyllables." The eloquence we have lost by using words worn out and lacking resonance, perhaps also by explaining and defining too much, may have been regained by artists. Through art, God constantly clears a path to our hearts. As Malraux noted, art carries "the ambition to rediscover and continue an obscurely eternal language which began in the depths of the ages." The Rothko Chapel is part of this endless address of man to the Divine.

If spiritual experience and silent worship belong fundamentally to the vocation of the Rothko Chapel, there is also another aspect. It is the search for togetherness, the building of communities of the heart, on the sister paths of ecumenism and human rights.

On February 27–28, 1971 the Rothko Chapel and the *Broken Obelisk* were solemnly dedicated by Christians (Orthodox, Catholics, Protestants), Jews and Muslims. From the start there was a guiding spirit: "the East and the West belong to God. Wherever we turn, there is God's face" (Qur'ān II:115). Two and a half years later (July 22–30, 1973) the colloquium "Traditional Modes of Contemplation and Action" assembled in the chapel Hindus, Buddhists, Jews, Christians, Muslims, interpreters of native American religion, and a practitioner of traditional religion from Africa. It was a landmark and it opened the way to future religious encounters. Four months later, at the insistence of Dom Helder Camara, another colloquium entitled "Human Rights/Human Reality" marked the chapel's involvement in human rights. Yet it was not until 1981 that a deliberate effort was made to dramatize the cause of human rights by instituting The Rothko Chapel Awards for Commitment to Truth and Freedom.

As one learns walking by walking, we are learning togetherness by meeting others. Lovingly. It is an effort to expand the soul. It does not imply a loss of identity or tradition. Quite the contrary. Sacred texts and holy men and women invite us to this conviviality.

In the Acts of the Apostles (10:34), Peter proclaims: "I see now how true it is that God has no favorites, but that in every nation the man who is God-fearing and does what is right is acceptable to Him." This matter-of-fact and rather naively expressed statement is the foundation stone for ecumenism. The stone is really a rock posed by God Himself: His love knows no barriers. Moved by this thought, Thomas Merton, four days before he died, at a meeting of contemplatives in Calcutta, asked everyone present to join hands and he said: "O God who taught us that you dwell in us when we open to one another, help us to keep that openness and to fight for it with all our strength."

Dominique de Menil

Rothko working in his studio, New York, ca. 1964

Foreword

Historical Context: Rothko, Newman, Johnson

Mark Rothko belongs to the generation of American artists born in the first decade of the century; his achievements span four decades, from the 1930s to the 1960s, centering on the middle of the century. By the 1960s, the vanguard art identified as Abstract Expressionism (a term with which both Mark Rothko and Barnett Newman were uncomfortable) had assumed a position of public prominence. Although hundreds of serious and talented artists were part of this collective endeavor, perhaps a dozen artists concern us most today. Of them, Rothko, Newman, Jackson Pollock and Clyfford Still most radically restructured the forms, methods and, in fact, the nature of what could constitute painting.

From the 1930s through the end of his life, Rothko's art evolved through four major phases. These can be identified as: paintings based on drawn and biomorphic images (1943–46); paintings composed of soft-edged, floating forms (1947–49); paintings with two or three realms of color arranged from top to bottom (the 1950s); and paintings of deepened palette and closely-hued colors within a more unified spatial realm (the 1960s). The transition from bicameral structures to a single encompassing color realm can be seen in the Rothko Chapel by comparing the south wall painting to the apse triptych. It is noteworthy that at the peak of interest in his more lyrical, sensuously-colored paintings from the 1950s, Rothko turned to an increasingly austere palette and explored the possibilities of painting in monochrome, venturing in advance of his audience into new areas of concern.

The transitions within Rothko's career are more overt than those of either Newman or Still, and different in kind from what occurs in Pollock's development. By the late 1940s Newman had uncovered the grand design of his life's work, which he carried forth through the 1950s and 1960s. The colored realms of space adumbrated in Rothko's paintings may be counterposed to Newman's work, where space is assertively declared and articulated by a vertical element. Newman's first sculpture was made in 1950. When he turned to sculpture again during the 1960s, *Broken Obelisk*, with its dramatic collision of the pyramid and inverted obelisk forms, was unique in his work and among the art of his peers, due to its implications of historical reference. Rothko's chapel paintings, on the other hand, carry no recognizable imagery. Despite their absolute iconoclasm, however, there is an underlying level of historical allusion implicit in the structural organization and configuration of parts within the ensemble; for instance, the octagonal plan of the chapel and the disposition of canvases into groupings, such as side wall and apse triptychs, are all iconographically resonant.

Philip Johnson, the original architect of the Rothko Chapel, at mid-century was one of the major proponents of rationalist modernism in twentieth-century architecture. Conceived by German, Dutch and American architects early in the century, modernism had indeed become an "International Style" in architecture by mid-century, and Philip Johnson became its crucial apologist and subsequent exemplar. Among the architects of his time, Johnson undoubtedly was closest to artists and the most empathetic to art of his time, by training, association and life pursuits. During the mid-1960s, however, when he began to collaborate with Rothko, Johnson was undergoing a period of transition from rational determinance to a more open and evocative architectural form, and his conflicts with Rothko over the design of the chapel would seem inevitable. Ultimately it was Rothko who made the key contribution to the chapel by insisting upon an octagonal plan. During the 1970s and 1980s, after Rothko and Newman had died, Johnson's architectural career re-emerged in a postmodernist style, embracing historical reprise and allusion.

An Heroic Resolution of Subject and Form

Among the American artists who emerged at mid-century—such as Rothko, Newman, Pollock and Still—was a shared ambition for art and for what art could mean, both *as* art and *beyond* art. Image and reference were reduced to the fundamental and the minimum, yet these artists were neither functionalists nor formalists. Rothko and Newman, in particular, claimed a metaphysical terrain for their art, Pollock and Still invoked the intrasubjective and the visionary, all of them embracing the hierarchy of transcendent values. Within the canons of mid-century iconoclasm, Rothko and Newman would appear to have most drastically purged their work of referential form; nevertheless, through the least articulation of means they sought to pose the broadest statements and questions of meaning, aspiring to an heroic resolution of subject and form.

Sanctuary

Rothko, Newman, Pollock and Still shared another important concern: each was looking for a new kind of locus for their art to be seen in the world, one that went beyond the topical associations of private and public collections, or ecclesiastical or institutional commissions. For Rothko, the chapel commission provided a long-sought opportunity to shape and control a total environment encompassing a group of paintings created for a specific space. Fortuitous circumstances brought Newman's *Broken Obelisk* to the chapel, but as an integral part of it. For our time, the Rothko Chapel comes closest to achieving a unique setting and philosophical context for an ensemble of art: it stands as a sanctuary for the work and workings of the human spirit, its agonies and aspirations.

Walter Hopps

Rothko in his 69th St. studio with chapel
paintings in progress, New York, 1965

Introduction

The Rothko Chapel in Houston is named for Mark Rothko, the American artist whose paintings hang inside the building. Originally planned for a Catholic university, but freed from any denominational ties before it was built, the chapel was dedicated on February 27, 1971 as "a sacred place open to all, every day."

Individuals and groups of all faiths come to the chapel—to meet, to celebrate, to pray. Colloquia have been held there since 1973, bringing together spiritual and intellectual leaders from around the world to discuss essential themes such as: traditional modes of contemplation and action in world religions; human rights; new strategies for development in the Third World; Islam and the quest for justice; and ethnicities and nations.[1] In 1981, to celebrate the tenth anniversary of the chapel, the Rothko Chapel Awards for Commitment to Truth and Freedom were inaugurated. Twelve individuals and groups were chosen that year, as were nine more at the fifteenth anniversary of the chapel in 1986.[2] On that occasion, the Carter-Menil Human Rights Prize was first awarded,[3] and an Oscar Romero prize was established.[4]

Rothko's paintings have helped to shape the destiny of the chapel as a place for private meditation, common worship and exchange of philosophical and religious insights. Many people have sensed an ambiance of somber tranquility which emanates from the paintings and is conducive to religious experience and meditation in the broadest sense of the word. The history of the Rothko Chapel as a living institution begins with its opening to the public on February 27, 1971. That history, which is being made daily as the chapel welcomes private visitors or hosts public events, is not our subject. Instead, this book is a history of how the chapel came into being.

The character of an institution is often stamped by the personalities of its founders. The chronicle of the conception and execution of the Rothko Chapel is very much about the individuals

Yuri Orlov accepting first Carter-Menil Human Rights Prize, *(left to right)*, Archbishop Desmond Tutu, Dr. Thompson Shannon, Yuri Orlov [with interpreter], Dominique de Menil, President Jimmy Carter, Rothko Chapel, December 10, 1986

involved: John and Dominique de Menil, who originated the commission in 1964; Mark Rothko, the painter; and Philip Johnson, the original architect. Each of these distinguished people brought his or her own ideas and expectations to the project; at times they were in harmony, at times in discord. The de Menils' friendship with Father Marie-Alain Couturier predisposed them to the idea of commissioning a church from a contemporary master. The project came to flower during their close association with the University of St. Thomas and in response to the untimely death of their friend Jermayne MacAgy, chairperson of the St. Thomas Art Department. Rothko belonged to a generation of artists who had taken American painting and sculpture to a monumental scale, and had previously created two environmental ensembles of paintings. The meaning he sought to convey in his paintings, while not specifically religious, was suited to a sacred place. Johnson was the initially selected architect not only for the chapel, but also for the buildings that would have surrounded it on its first projected site at the University of St. Thomas; his designs therefore embodied his ideas for the total scheme of the campus.

The background sections of this history are intended to elucidate the factors that helped to shape the attitudes of the participants toward the commission. The architecture is discussed concurrently with the making of the paintings, and separately in a section tracing the evolution of the design in Johnson's hands for two years, and subsequently with Howard Barnstone and Eugene Aubry of Houston, who completed the building. Barnett Newman's sculpture *Broken Obelisk,* purchased by the de Menils, was placed outside the chapel and dedicated to Martin Luther King, Jr. The sculpture is discussed here as an integral part of the chapel complex and its history.

Rothko's paintings are the heart of this history; the largest part of the narrative is therefore devoted to him and to his murals. The cooperation of Rothko's friends and the artists who assisted him has brought forth much previously unknown information about how the paintings were made. In addition, drawings and paintings relating to the Chapel that were in the artist's collection at his death have been included here to illuminate different stages of his thought.

Notes

1. "Traditional Modes of Contemplation and Action" was held in July 1973; "Human Rights/Human Reality" in December 1973; "Toward a New Strategy for Development" in February 1977; "Islam: Spiritual Message and Quest for Justice" in October 1981; and "Ethnicities and Nations" in October 1983. The proceedings of three of the colloquia have been published: *Contemplation and Action in World Religions,* edited by Yusuf Ibish and Ileana Marculescu, (Seattle and London: University of Washington Press, 1977); *Toward a New Strategy for Development* (New York: Pergamon Press, 1979); and *Ethnicities and Nations: Processes of Inter-Ethnic Relations in Latin America, South-East Asia and the Pacific,* edited by Remo Guidieri, Francesco Pellizzi, and Stanley J. Tambiah (Austin: University of Texas Press, 1988).

2. The 1981 Rothko Chapel Awards went to: Giuseppe Alberigo, Bologna; Amadou Hampaté Bâ, Abidjan; Balys Gajauskas, U.S.S.R.; Douglas and Joan Grant, Berkeley; Las Madres de la Plaza de Mayo, Buenos Aires; Ned O'Gorman, New York; Warren Robbins, Washington, D.C.; Sakokwenonkwas (Chief Tom Porter), The Mohawk Nation at Akwesasne, Raquette Point, New York; Zwelakhe Sisulu, Johannesburg; Roberto Cuellar, Socorro Juridico, San Salvador; Tatiana Velikanova, U.S.S.R.; José Zalaquett, Chile. In 1986, the recipients were: Charter 77, Prague; Myles Horton, Tennessee; Helen Joseph, Johannesburg; Anatoly Koryagin, U.S.S.R.; Jonathan Kuttab, Occupied West Bank; Leonidas Eduardo Proaño Villalba, Ecuador; Sanctuary, worldwide; Raja Shehadeh, Occupied West Bank; and Albertina Sisulu, South Africa.

3. On March 19, 1986 The Carter-Menil Human Rights Foundation was formed. That same year on December 10, the anniversary of The Universal Declaration of Human Rights of the United Nations, the first Carter-Menil Human Rights Prize was shared by two recipients: Yuri Orlov, Soviet physicist and co-founder of the Moscow Helsinki Group; and the Group for Mutual Support, an association of Guatemalan mothers and wives of "disappeared" persons. The prizes were presented at the Rothko Chapel in a joint ceremony with the Rothko Chapel awards for Truth and Freedom. The second Carter-Menil Human Rights Prize was awarded to La Vicaria de la Solidaridad, Chile; the presentation took place at the Carter Presidential Center in Atlanta on December 10, 1987.

4. The Oscar Romero Award was established by 1986 by the Rothko Chapel. The first recipient was Leonidas Eduardo Proaño Villalba, retired Bishop of Riobamba, Ecuador. In 1988 Paulo Evaristo Cardinal Arns was chosen to receive this award.

The magnitude, on every level of experience and meaning, of the task in which you have involved me, exceeds all my preconceptions. And it is teaching me to extend myself beyond what I thought was possible for me.

For this I thank you

Mark Rothko

Excerpt from a letter to Dominique and John de Menil, January 1, 1966

Background

Mark Rothko, ca. 1949

Background:
Mark Rothko

There is no such thing as a good painting about nothing. . . . the subject is crucial and only that subject matter is valid which is timeless and tragic. [5]

Mark Rothko

Marcus Rothkowitz, born in 1903, was a Russian Jew whose family emigrated to Portland, Oregon in his youth. He had taken art classes during high school, and was especially interested in music, literature, mathematics and the theater—propensities which would all contribute to the character of his painting. After two years of study at Yale University, he moved to New York. In one account, Rothko indicated that he became an artist almost by chance. But on another occasion he declared that he did so because he wanted to raise painting to the level of poignancy of music and poetry.

Rothko's commitment to content in the work of art is clear throughout his career. This was manifest in the titles he gave to paintings in the 1940s, such as *Entombment, Prehistoric Memory, Ritual (fig. 1), The Source (fig. 2)*. During that decade Rothko explored mythic themes: he was in search of "eternal symbols . . . to express basic psychological ideas." [6] Although stylized, his images from the early 1940s contain recognizable human forms; in the middle of the decade, however, they become more biomorphic than human. By 1947 Rothko had essentially abandoned all reference to recognizable imagery, and in 1950 arrived at an arrangement of abstract forms which he would use and refine for the rest of his life: one or more roughly rectangular color forms, usually horizontal, floated on a background color. With his radically reduced visual means, Rothko meant to heighten rather than lessen the importance of subject. In fact, in 1948–1949 he participated with Barnett Newman, Clyfford Still, William Baziotes,

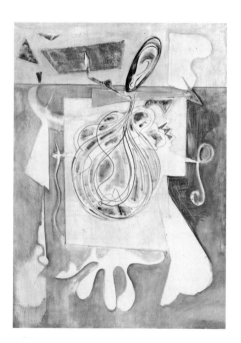

1. Mark Rothko
Ritual, 1944
Oil and pencil on canvas
53⅞ × 39½ in.
Walker Art Center, Minneapolis;
  gift of The Mark Rothko Foundation

David Hare, and Robert Motherwell—all of them artists involved with abstraction—in founding a school on Eighth Street in New York. At Newman's suggestion, the school took its name from a principal theme of discussion, The Subjects of the Artist.

Rothko and a few contemporaries dared to commit themselves to the expression of "timeless" ideas, emotions, and truths through abstract forms and painterly means alone. This is one of the ways in which we may understand Rothko's aspiration to invest painting with the affective power of a purely abstract medium like music.

About the time that Rothko removed all referential images from his painting, he also abandoned allusive titles for the works. Instead, they were given numbers, or descriptive titles referring to their colors (*fig. 3*). This meant that he had to convey his sense of subject to the viewer by the purely formal means of painting—the size of the canvas, the proportion and scale of the forms, colors of forms and of ground, and the quality of his brushstroke—without even the hint that a title might offer. By eliminating titles, he removed the last concrete reference to anything outside the painting. He left himself and his viewer to confront the work of art, unaided and unhindered. In 1952 he wrote:

> The progression of a painter's work, as it travels in time from point to point, will be toward clarity: toward the elimination of all obstacles between the painter and the idea; and the idea and the observer. As examples of such obstacles, I give (among others) memory, history, or geometry, which are swamps of generalizations from which one might pull out parodies of ideas (which are ghosts) but never an idea itself. To achieve this clarity is, inevitably, to be understood.[7]

Rothko made great demands of himself and of his audience, and he was not always understood. He had to make clear to the public that by simplifying his compositions of subtly-colored forms, he was not merely making a formal statement. In an interview published in 1957, when he was complimented on the beauty of his color harmonies, he exploded in protest:

> I'm not interested in relationships of color or form or anything else. . . . I'm interested only in expressing basic human emotions—tragedy, ecstasy, doom, and so on—and the fact that lots of people break down and cry when confronted with my pictures shows that I *communicate* these basic human emotions. . . . The people who weep before my pictures are having the same religious experience I had when I painted them, and if you, as you say, are moved only by their color relationships, then you miss the point![8]

2. Mark Rothko
The Source, 1947
Oil on canvas
39⅝ × 28 in.
The National Gallery of Art, Wash., D.C.;
    gift of The Mark Rothko Foundation

3. Mark Rothko
The Green Stripe, 1955
Oil on canvas
67 × 54 in.
The Menil Collection, Houston

Throughout most of the 1950s Rothko's paintings were aston-ishing visions of color, yet he steadfastly denied he was a colorist. His œuvre was dominated at that time by pulsating reds, yellows, oranges, pinks—colors that seem to throb with life and joy, but with which he claimed he wanted to express tragedy. To one ob-server who hailed such works as "celebrations," Rothko remarked that they were also the colors of an inferno. [9]

Beginning in the late 1950s, somber, darker color appeared in Rothko's palette. In the canvases of the early 1960s, the bright hues gave way with greater frequency to blues, browns, plums, maroons, and black. For all of his mural series, beginning with the paintings intended for the Seagram Building in 1958–1959, Rothko chose a somber palette of few colors—partly perhaps in response to working on an architectural scale.[10] Throughout the decade of the 1960s he often worked with reduced and darker colors in his easel paintings as well, until in his late work bright color seems mostly to disappear from his palette. Rothko's last paintings, magnificent works, are simple rectangles of gray next to rectangles of black or brown.

◆　　　　　◆　　　　　◆

No possible program notes can explain our paintings. Their explanation must come out of a consummated experience between picture and onlooker. The appreciation of art is a true marriage of minds.[11]

Rothko was always extremely attentive to the way his paintings were shown. His conviction was such that, even before he became successful, when exhibitions would have helped him become better known, on at least one occasion he refused to let his paintings travel in a circulating exhibition where he could not personally oversee their installation. He was particularly concerned with how his paintings were lighted, insisting on dim rather than strong light. He knew the conditions under which the subtle color relationships could speak most affectively.

Philip Guston remembers the time when he and Rothko went to see the installation of one of Rothko's shows at Janis Gallery [New York] (fig. 4). They strolled into the gallery and Mark, without a word, switched off half the lights. When Sidney Janis emerged from his office, the three of them chatted a bit and, in a pause in the conversation, Janis slid off and turned all the lights back on. Rothko didn't say anything. They finished their visit; Janis went back to work, Guston and Rothko waited for the elevator, and just before they entered it, Rothko turned half the lights back off again. "I'm positive," Guston says, "that Mark sneaked up there every day and turned the lights down—without ever complaining or explaining."[12]

As Katharine Kuh observed, Rothko knew that low light would reveal the most subtle vibrations of the color.[13] He felt that too much light washed out color intensity. Whenever he could, Rothko supervised the hanging of his paintings for private collectors, always insisting on reduced lighting.[14] His preoccupation with the way the paintings were displayed and lighted may at times have seemed eccentric, even obsessive, but it was grounded in a conviction that he expressed quite movingly in a now-famous quote:

A picture lives by companionship, expanding and quickening in the eyes of the sensitive observer. It dies by the same token. It is therefore a risky act to send it out into the world. How often it must be impaired by the eyes of the unfeeling and the cruelty of the impotent who would extend their affliction universally! [15]

Given this outlook, it is clear that the chance to create an environmental ensemble of paintings for a defined space would appeal to Rothko. Like his contemporaries among American painters—Pollock, Still, Newman, Motherwell—Rothko worked on a large scale. He explained this in a seeming paradox: "I paint large pictures because I want to create a state of intimacy. A large picture is an immediate transaction; it takes you into it." [16] This effect would be still further enhanced by an environmental group of paintings. Herbert Ferber, the sculptor, recalls frequently discussing the possibility of such environmental installations with Rothko in the late 1950s. Rothko already had a pet project: "He wanted to find a sponsor who would build a little house in New York with Rothko's name on it where his paintings would be seen without having to

4. Mark Rothko exhibition (installation view), Sidney Janis Gallery, New York, 1958

5. Chapel of the Rosary at Vence, France (interior), showing Henri Matisse's *Virgin and Child (left)* and *Stations of the Cross (right)*, 1951

confuse them with the works of other people."[17] Rothko expanded on that idea when he explained it to Mrs. Gifford Phillips; saying that he didn't approve of large museums, Rothko proposed a series of one-man museums in

> small, very simple buildings—made of cinder block, I remember that—scattered throughout the country in small towns. And each building would be an homage to a particular artist. One would contain Reinhardts, one Rothkos . . .[18]

In the circle of artists that included Rothko, the idea of an environmental ensemble is first articulated in a letter from Clyfford Still to Betty Parsons in 1949. Regarding paintings he had sent for an exhibition, Still wrote,

> These works are a series of acts best comprehended in groups or as a continuity. Except as a created revelation, a new experience, they are without value. It is my desire that they be kept in groups as much as possible and remain so. . . . So I am in the strange position of seeking an environment for the work and the small means wherein I'll be free to continue the "act."[19]

Still and Rothko had secular environments in mind. However, the first opportunity for work of this scale was a religious commission: their colleagues Motherwell, Gottlieb, and Ferber each created a large-scale work for the B'nai Israel Synagogue in New Jersey in 1951. Also in that year, the dedication in southern France of the

Chapel of the Rosary at Vence, with its interior created and supervised in every detail by Henri Matisse, must have stimulated all of them *(fig. 5)*. Matisse's chapel is known to have been of great interest to Jackson Pollock, whose own unrealized projects include a chapel. [20]

In 1958–1959, Herbert Ferber developed the concept of making a sculptural environment. Again, he remembers exchanging ideas frequently with Rothko, who during that same period was at work on his first group of mural paintings, commissioned by Philip Johnson for the Four Seasons restaurant which he had designed for the German architect Ludwig Mies van der Rohe's new Seagram Building in New York. [21] De Kooning saw Rothko shortly after this commission had been confirmed:

> He was very happy. . . .This was the first time that he was making one painting in relation to another painting. . . . Like . . . writing different chapters in a novel . . . to relate one to the other, to get a unity, a whole work. [22]

The Seagram commission afforded Rothko his first opportunity for a permanent installation of a group of his paintings. With it came another challenge: to create a cycle of works united by common thematic elements. For the first time he had to orchestrate an ensemble of paintings whose meaning would unfold in time and space, in the relationship of each painting to the others. Not surprisingly, Rothko unconsciously sought inspiration in architecture. The project was well underway when he realized that he had been trying to create a sense of enclosure not unlike Michelangelo's Laurentian Library in Florence. [23]

◆   ◆   ◆

In 1947, Rothko had written of his paintings as "dramas." [24] With the Seagram murals, he first used his full powers as a master of dramatic effect on a monumental scale *(fig. 6)*. In his studio on the Bowery, he had scaffolding installed to simulate the restaurant's interior. He worked impassionedly, painting numerous canvases from among which he could select those that would form the most powerful arrangement. Dan Rice and Dore Ashton both recall Rothko's experimenting with a variety of schemes until he got the results that he wanted. [25]

Once the murals were completed, however, he refused to deliver them. According to Katherine Kuh, he had visited the newly-opened restaurant, first with his wife Mel, then a day or two later

6. Mark Rothko
Mural panel from the Seagram Building
   commission, 1958
Oil on canvas
105 in. × 144 in.
The Tate Gallery, London

with Ms. Kuh herself. He told Ms. Kuh he had realized that this major work of his would be merely a decorative backdrop for the tastes and transactions of a society he abhorred.[26]

This decision took enormous moral and financial courage. Rothko had devoted more than a year's work to the project, and although he was increasingly well known at that time, he was by no means well off. Defaulting on the commission might also have cost him his only chance to realize an environmental installation, and he hoped to find another client who would purchase the murals. Museum curator Douglas MacAgy and his former wife Jermayne had known Rothko since the late 1940s, when they had met at the California School of Fine Arts in San Francisco where Rothko taught painting at Clyfford Still's invitation in the summers of 1947 and 1949. Douglas MacAgy suggested that his friends Dominique and John de Menil visit Rothko's studio on the Bowery to view the paintings.

MacAgy thought that the murals might be appropriate for a chapel at the University of St. Thomas—a small Catholic liberal arts college in Houston directed by the Basilian Fathers, whose academic programs and campus the de Menils were helping to build; he knew that Philip Johnson's master plan for the college included a large chapel, as yet unbuilt. Dominique and John de Menil had never previously met Mark Rothko, but they were no strangers to his work. Although they had started collecting when they moved to America in 1941, by 1960 the French-born couple had begun to assemble a collection that embraced a broad scope of history, and that already included three paintings by Rothko. When they saw the Seagram murals, the de Menils "were overwhelmed by the power and passion of these great, somber murals. . . To their astonishment they realized they were speaking in whispers."[27]

Notes

5. Mark Rothko and Adolph Gottlieb, letter to Edward Alden Jewell, Art Editor, *The New York Times,* June 7, 1943.

6. Rothko and Gottlieb, 1943.

7. In the catalogue of the exhibition *15 Americans, 1952,* p. 18.

8. Rodman, 1957, pp. 93–94.

9. A statement made to Arnold Glimcher, recounted by Mr. Glimcher to Dominique de Menil, 1979 (interview).

10. Dan Rice, Rothko's assistant on the Seagram paintings, suggested that the reduction of color there had to do with Rothko's concern with architecture

(Dan Rice, interviewed by Arnold Glimcher in the catalogue of the exhibition *The 1958–59 Murals: Second Series,* 1978, n.p.). See also Eliza Rathbone's fine study of Rothko's series (1978, especially pp. 245–269).

11. Rothko and Gottlieb, 1943.

12. Hess, 1970, p. 29.

13. Kuh, 1981 (interview).

14. As he did for Vera and Donald Blinken. See Davidson, 1982, pp. 110–131. I am grateful to Elsian Cozens for bringing this article to my attention.

15. *15 Americans,* p. 18.

16. Rothko, 1958 (lecture); noted by Dore Ashton, from *Cimaise,* December 1958, reprinted in *New York School. The First Generation,* (1971, p. 143).

17. Herbert Ferber, 1981 (interview).

18. Letter from Mrs. Gifford Phillips to Dominique de Menil, November 17, 1972.

19. Quoted in Alloway, 1973, p. 39. See Ashton (1983, pp. 92–98) on the relations between Still and Rothko.

20. E.A. Carmean, Jr., "The Church Project: Pollock's Passion Themes," *Art in America,* Summer 1982, pp. 100–122.

21. Ferber, 1981 (interview).

22. Liss, 1979, p. 43.

23. Fischer, 1970, p. 16. In the late 1950s, Ferber had discussed the Laurentian Library with Rothko because of his own interest as a sculptor in the relationship between art and architecture in an environment (December 1983 [conversation with the author]).

24. Rothko, 1947–1948.

25. Dan Rice in *The 1958–59 Murals: Second Series,* 1978, n. p.; Dore Ashton, October 1986 (personal communication). Rothko told John Fischer that he had painted three separate mural series (Fischer, 1971, p. 16). At this writing, however, it seems doubtful that the exact components of those series can be identified.

26. Kuh, 1981 (interview), reading from the manuscript of her memoirs about Rothko. For recollections on the commission from other sources, see Alley, 1981, pp. 658–659.

27. Snell, 1971, p. 52.

Background:
Dominique and John de Menil

J ohn de Menil was born in Paris in 1904.[28] As a teenager, he dropped out of school and took a clerical job in a bank. He soon decided to complete his studies, however, and he did it with the same intelligence, energy and determination that he showed all his life: finishing his *baccalauréat* and graduate work in political science and law while working full time in the bank with increasing responsibilities. At the age of twenty, he and five other promising young men were awarded travel fellowships that took them on a freighter from Marseilles to Ceylon, Australia, Tahiti, and the Panama Canal. In 1925–1926, he renounced his officer's commission, choosing instead to do his military service as an infantryman in the Rif Mountains during the Moroccan Tribal Wars. By the time he married in 1931, he was in charge of the financial department of one of France's leading investment banks. In 1939 he joined Les Procédés Schlumberger, moving to America with the company's operations during the war.

Dominique Schlumberger was born in 1908, the second of three daughters, and grew up in Paris. Although the Schlumberger family was Protestant, her parents Conrad and Louise were agnostic. Her parents were not art collectors, but even as a girl Dominique revealed that aspect of her nature: she collected fossils, stamps, butterflies, matchboxes. . . . During her youth, her father (joined in 1920 by his brother Marcel) conducted pioneering experiments in geophysics, developing and perfecting the highly sophisticated techniques of electrical measurement that would make Schlumberger, Ltd. a leading firm in worldwide petroleum exploration.

7. John and Dominique de Menil, 1971

Dominique, who also had a scientific bent, pursued graduate studies in physics and mathematics at the Sorbonne. She met John de Menil at a party which neither had wanted to attend; they talked together the whole evening, and married a year later. In 1932 Dominique de Menil became a Catholic, and in January 1936 she attended the Week of Prayer for Christian Unity at the Sacred Heart Basilica, Montmartre, where Father Congar delivered a series of homilies on ecumenism that were to become the basis of his book *Divided Christendom: Principles of a Catholic Ecumenism*—a landmark. She was deeply impressed.[29]

Dominique and John de Menil *(fig. 7)* discovered their passion for art when in America during the mid-1940s under the guidance of another Dominican, Father Marie-Alain Couturier *(fig. 8)*.[30] Father Couturier is justly famous for his role during the late 1940s and early 1950s in the realization of the four great modern religious monuments of France: the churches at Assy *(fig. 9)* and Audincourt *(fig. 10)*, which contain works by Georges Braque, Fernand Léger, Jacques Lipschitz and Georges Rouault, among others; the Matisse chapel at Vence *(fig. 11)*; and Le Corbusier's church at Ronchamp. The de Menils had first met Couturier in France before World War II. As fate would have it, Couturier was caught on American shores when France fell to the Germans in 1940, and spent the war years in New York in relative seclusion except for occasional trips to Canada. His contacts with expatriate artists, his frequent gallery and museum visits in New York, and most of all meeting Henri Laugier, deepened his understanding of

8. Father Couturier, 1950

modern art. Laugier was a man of science and a passionate connoisseur of modern art who became friends with Couturier after hearing him lecture on Picasso. Laugier was then at the United Nations as assistant secretary general for social affairs, the highest post held by a Frenchman at the U.N.[31]

Whenever the de Menils visited New York in 1943–1945 they saw Father Couturier, and with him they visited exhibitions and art dealers, making their first art purchases. After the war, the de Menils met Father Couturier on their annual summer vacations in France. By then, he had embarked on projects to engage important modern artists to work for churches in France. His goal was nothing less than

> to bring to an end, by means of a direct achievement, the absurd divorce which for the past century has separated the church from living art. . . . to appeal to the greatest of independent artists, no matter what might be their personal convictions.[32]

In the summer of 1952, he took the de Menils to see Assy, Audincourt, Vence, and the site at Ronchamp where Le Corbusier was going to build *(figs. 12, 13)*. Mrs. de Menil's impressions of the trip were published in *l'Art Sacré* the following spring. To read her thoughts on seeing Assy is to seize the fresh conviction and excitement generated by the experience:

> Everyone agrees that Assy is a milestone in the history of religious art, but some criticize this thing, others that. As for me, I can't criticize. . . . What does it matter if it isn't perfect? The child is born: he will grow!

9. Church of Notre-Dame-de-Toute Grâce, Assy, France (facade), showing Ferdinand Léger's *The Virgin of the Litany*, 1950

10. Audincourt (interior), showing Ferdinand Léger's stainglass windows

11. Chapel of the Rosary at Vence, France, consecration, with Father Couturier *(left)*, June 25, 1951

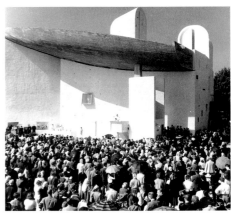

12. Le Corbusier, Ronchamp Chapel, (interior south wall), France, 1950-55

13. Le Corbusier, Ronchamp Chapel, (exterior), France, 1950-55

The following passage was written by Father Couturier and inserted in her article:

> It is said "one only baptizes life," yet for so long in Christian countries we have stubbornly persisted in baptizing just mummies and the dead. What enormous stillborn structures St. Patrick's of New York and St. John the Divine are! Then again, if I think of all that is done in the U.S.A. in the name of a better "philosophy of Christian art," of all this sickening triumph of imitation modern, of these pseudo-naïve statues or others full of sentimental piety, if I even think of what I just saw in Rome herself (Sacro-Cuore, Sant'Eugenio!), I can only regard with emotion what was born here: this modest Bonnard, Léger's mosaic, these Rouaults and Bazaines, this little Braque, this drawing of Matisse. . . .
>
> Let's forget the rest, and hope that year by year works that are purer still will take their place.[33]

Douglas MacAgy knew of the de Menils' interest in obtaining the finest contemporary art and architecture for churches when he proposed that they consider the Seagram murals for a chapel at the University of St. Thomas, Houston. But in 1960, when they had first visited Rothko's studio and were shown the murals, the time was not yet right; St. Thomas already had an exquisite small chapel made by a gifted student, Glen Heim, to meet its needs while the more urgently required labs and classrooms were being built. Furthermore, the Seagram murals had been conceived for a specific space, and it seemed problematic to have to reconcile that arrangement with the architecture of a chapel not yet commissioned. Nevertheless, Dominique de Menil made a second visit to Rothko's studio, accompanied by Father Flahiff, then the Superior of the Basilians, to consider the possibilities. When the de Menils finally decided against it, in their minds they had merely postponed the project.

Notes

28. The following biographical information is drawn from the four-part article by Marguerite Johnston, 1977; from Anne Gruner Schlumberger, (1982); and from conversations between Dominique de Menil and the author. See also Freed, l984, and Glueck, 1986.

John de Menil was christened Jean, but anglicized the spelling of his first name when he was naturalized an American citizen. He died in 1973.

29. Father Congar was born in France in 1904. After completing his studies at the Dominican seminary of Le Saulchoir and becoming a priest, he decided to devote himself to the question of the division between Christians—a problem that had not been addressed by theologians since Moehler and Newman. In 1937, Congar published *Chrétiens désunis—Principes d'un "œcuménisme" catholique* (English ed., *Divided Christendom: Principles of a Catholic "Ecumenism,"* 1939). The work, which had been over five years in the making, brought a new approach: reconciliation between Christians could not be achieved by apologetics; knowledge, and understanding of each others' position were prerequisites. This important book contributed greatly to the ecumenical movement among Catholics. After four years in a German prison camp, Congar resumed his scholarly life at the Saulchoir monastery, the center of Dominican studies that had been transferred from Belgium to Soisy, outside of Paris. But, in a climate of emerging integrism, tense with suspicion, Father Congar was misunderstood and attacked. He was exiled from Paris and forbidden to teach or write. The tide turned with the election of John XXIII as Pope. Asked by Cardinal Marty to be his theological advisor at the Council, Congar soon became one of the influential theologians of Vatican II, where he actively participated in the drafting of documents on the church, ecumenism, the priesthood, missions, and the church's role in the modern world. (See Jean Puyo's interview with Father Congar, *Le Centurion,* 1975; and Komonchak, 1983, pp. 402–405).

30. Couturier's diary (or chronicles: "chroniques") has recently been edited by Marcel Billot and published under the title *La Vérité Blessée* (Paris: Plon, 1984). The entries for the year 1952 (pp. 283–311) are particularly rich in references to the artists Bazaine, Matisse, Braque, et. al. It was during this year that Couturier and the de Menils made their pilgrimage to see the new monuments of the Catholic Church in France. Mrs. de Menil's quotation of Le Corbusier, "Je crois à la peau des choses," is cited on July 7, 1953 (p. 294 and p. 294 n. 2).

31. Henri Laugier was assistant secretary general to the United Nations from 1946 to 1951. See his obituary in *The New York Times,* January 21, l973, p. 60, cols. 5–6.

32. Couturier, 1951, p. 30.

33. D. de Menil, 1953, pp. 12–14.

14. Mark Rothko room (installation view),
The Phillips Collection, Washington,
D.C., ca. 1960

15. Mark Rothko, Seagram Building
commission murals, 1958 as installed
at The Tate Gallery, London, ca. 1970

Background:
1960–1964

The Seagram murals were not to find a home until the end of the decade, when Rothko gave nine of the paintings to The Tate Gallery in London *(fig. 15)*. [34] But several projects in the early 1960s kept Rothko thinking about and engaged in environmental installations of his work. The first of these arose when Duncan Phillips decided to devote a room to Rothko's work in the new wing of the Phillips Collection in Washington, D.C., opening in November 1960 *(fig. 14)*. [35] Phillips had already mounted two temporary exhibitions with paintings by Rothko—a group exhibition in early 1957 which probably included one gallery where only Rothko's work was hung, and a one-person exhibition in May 1960. [36] Phillips had purchased two paintings from the 1957 exhibition, and two more in 1960. [37]

Unfortunately, nothing is known of the discussions that might have taken place between Duncan Phillips and Rothko concerning the arrangements for the room in the new building. Phillips, who was known for his sensitive installations of works of art, may not have sought Rothko's advice at all. When Arthur Hall Smith visited the Phillips' home in 1959 to interview for a position at the Phillips Collection, Mr. and Mrs. Phillips proudly showed him a model of the Rothko room, which Duncan Phillips likened to a chapel. [38] The gray wall color and the low lighting levels gave the room a different character than the others in the new building. Rothko came to visit the installation in January 1961, when he was in Washington to attend the Kennedy inauguration. Smith accompanied Rothko to the gallery that day, and recalls that the artist was favorably impressed with the installation, but couldn't resist making some adjustments in the juxtaposition and lighting of the paintings.[39] We know from friends and collaborators of Rothko's that he was so enthusiastic about the wall color and the lighting of his works at the Phillips that he used them on at least one occasion as an example for future exhibitions.[40] The fact that Duncan Phillips' installation has remained essentially intact is all the more important by virtue of being the only extant installation of Rothko's paintings seen and endorsed by the artist himself.

In 1961, The Museum of Modern Art mounted a major exhibition of Rothko's work. Peter Selz, the museum curator responsible for the exhibition, worked closely with Rothko throughout the project, from the selection of work and the design of the space to the hanging and lighting of the paintings *(fig. 16)*. He recalls that the room at the Phillips collection served them as a model.[41] Again, Rothko was very concerned with wall color and the lighting of the works. According to Wilder Green, then head of the exhibition program at The Museum of Modern Art, Rothko was anxious that his work not be perceived as decorative or pretty.[42] He resisted the standard formula of white walls and bright light, settling on pale gray walls with lighting levels well below those normally used. When The Museum of Modern Art sent the exhibition on a tour of European museums, Rothko mailed written installation instructions to the Whitechapel Gallery in London.[43]

16. Mark Rothko Retrospective (installation view), The Museum of Modern Art, New York, 1961

In 1961 Rothko also received his second mural commission through the initiative of Wassily Leontief, a Nobel laureate in economics and friend of the artist.[44] Professor Leontief suggested to his associates in the Society of Fellows at Harvard University that they ask Rothko to create paintings for their new room in the penthouse of the Holyoke Center, designed by José Luis Sert. Rothko accepted, and during 1961–1962 painted a triptych and two individual canvases, which he donated to Harvard *(figs. 17, 18)*. The room where they were to hang had been already designed, but Rothko became very involved in decisions about the finishing details.[45] He called in Wilder Green, with whom he had previously worked on The Museum of Modern Art installation, as a consultant.[46] Together they choose a greenish gray fabric to cover the walls and devised the best lighting system possible within the constraints of the building. Green remembers that the space was low, inflexible, and crowded with tables and chairs; neither he nor Rothko was very satisfied with the final results. When Dore Ashton accompanied Rothko to see the paintings in the Holyoke Center, he expressed his concern about the potential damage to them from light which poured in from windows at either end of the long penthouse.[47] This risk was compounded when the university administration decided to rent the space for a variety of campus functions, instead of reserving it for gatherings of the Society of Fellows as originally intended. Rothko's choice and handling of materials for the murals decisively contributed to their vulnerability.[48] The

17. Mark Rothko
Mural for Holyoke Center (detail),
  1961–62
Oil and glue on unprimed canvas
105¼ in. × 180 in.
The Harvard University, Cambridge, Mass.,
  Gift of Mark Rothko

18. Mark Rothko
Mural for Holyoke Center (detail),
  1961–62
Oil and glue on unprimed canvas
105¼ in. × 394 in. (triptych)
The Harvard University, Cambridge, Mass.,
  Gift of Mark Rothko

eventual deterioration of the paintings led to the decision, made in 1979 in consultation with the Rothko Foundation, to remove the murals from the Holyoke Center and place them in safekeeping at the Fogg Art Museum until they could be installed in an appropriate space. [49]

Between 1960 and 1964—while Rothko was involved in these projects of the Phillips Collection, The Museum of Modern Art, and the murals at Harvard—the de Menils continued to pursue their interests in Houston, New York, and Paris, becoming United States citizens in 1962. Along with his responsibilities at Schlumberger, Ltd., John de Menil was very active on the boards of The Museum of Modern Art and the Museum of Primitive Art in New York, the Institute of International Education, Houston and Sarah Lawrence College.

Since the late 1940s, the de Menils had devoted their energies to bringing important art to Houston. Early members of the city's Contemporary Arts Association, in 1951 John de Menil and his wife wrote hundreds of letters to organize an exhibition of twenty-four works by Van Gogh, borrowed from American collections. In 1955 the de Menils were also instrumental in bringing Dr. Jermayne MacAgy to Houston as the first professional director of the Contemporary Arts Association. [50]

Jermayne MacAgy *(fig. 19)* had worked at the California Palace of the Legion of Honor museum in San Francisco from 1941 to

1955, serving variously as Assistant and Acting Director from 1943 and installing an extraordinary number of exhibitions each year. Her work there was praised by Alfred Frankenstein in the *San Francisco Chronicle:* "There is probably no museum in the United States where the art of displaying art has been developed to so fine a pitch."[51] Her genius for exhibition display came to enchant and inform Houston's growing museum-going public.

Among the de Menils' most important contributions to Houston during the 1950s and 1960s was their role in the development of the University of St. Thomas. Approached by St. Thomas professor Father Sullivan to assist the university in its building program, John de Menil explained the advantages of choosing an internationally known architect to design the campus, and suggested three or four architects, offering to make a gift of a master plan for the campus if such a decision were reached. The university's governing board chose Philip Johnson *(fig. 21)*, who was to become one of America's foremost architects of skyscrapers in the 1970s and 1980s, and whose office towers would feature significantly in Houston's downtown and satellite skylines. At the time he was commissioned by St. Thomas, Johnson was known for his smaller buildings in the modernist International Style largely deriving from the work of the German architect Mies van der Rohe. Among these were the de Menils' house in Houston, designed by Johnson in 1948–1949 concurrently with his own house in New Canaan, Connecticut—a Miesian jewel known as the "Glass House"—and the Boissonnas

20. *Islands Beyond* (installation view), Jones Hall, University of St. Thomas, 1962

house in 1956, also in New Canaan *(fig. 22)*. In 1951 Johnson had served as architect for the corporate offices of Schlumberger, Ltd. in Ridgefield, Connecticut.

Once the St. Thomas master plan was designed in 1957, Dominique and John de Menil became involved with other aspects of the developing university. They gave funds for teaching positions in French, economics and classics, and helped recruit faculty. They also pledged to underwrite the art department, persuading Jermayne MacAgy to become its founding chairman in 1959. As Director of Houston's Contemporary Arts Association from 1955 to 1959, she organized an active exhibitions program, including a one-person exhibition of Rothko's work in 1957. The de Menils felt certain she was the right person to launch an original and dynamic program for the university.

At St. Thomas, Jermayne MacAgy worked as a curator, teacher, and public lecturer, deftly staging provocative thematic exhibitions that brought together works from different cultures and historical periods *(fig. 20)*, as well as mounting exhibitions devoted to the art of her time. In all crucial respects, the interests of the de Menils were congruent with those of Jermayne MacAgy. Working closely with them, she helped to assemble systematic collections of tribal art and antiquities to function as a teaching collection for students in the art department. Her lectures combined scholarly research with imaginative insights, captivating her students as well as a large audience from the Houston community. She was an academic who inspired a non-academic public. Adventurous, tenacious, precise, witty and insightful—she was simply unique. Upon her untimely death at the age of fifty on February 18, 1964, the de Menils, the university, and the community of her followers were all bereft.

After MacAgy's death, the de Menils' plan for a university museum at St. Thomas lost its meaning. Faced with abandoning cherished projects, Dominique de Menil responded, "When the floor collapses, it's time to make an act of faith."[52] They went to university president Father Murphy and proposed building a chapel at St. Thomas, as the Basilian fathers had wanted from the beginning. Philip Johnson would design the structure, and the de Menils would ask Mark Rothko to create paintings for the interior. Rothko was a natural choice, having been a friend of Jermayne MacAgy. Most importantly, the de Menils recalled the extraordinary paintings he had created for the Seagram Building, and the artist's intense interest in creating an ambient ensemble of paintings.

21. Philip Johnson, 1960

On April 17, 1964 Dominique de Menil went to call on Mark Rothko, accompanied by Louise Ferrari, another close friend and collaborator of Jermayne MacAgy.

> I asked him if he would consider making paintings for the Catholic chapel we were going to build at the University of St. Thomas. He said yes and seemed very happy. The meeting was simple. He said he would devote all his time to the project. Figures were never advanced. He just said that Bernard Reis would write to us about that.[53]

◆   ◆   ◆

Though the arena for the artist is now the secular world, he undertakes his task with the dedication of spirit which in other eras was the mark of the priest and the seer.[54]

Jane Dillenberger

Rothko once told Dominique de Menil that he had been very religious as a young child, dragging his mother to the synagogue several times a day, more time than even a devout woman could spare. However, his life in America did not include practice of the Jewish faith, nor did he have any direct experience of the Catholic religion. Yet like many artists in our secular society, Rothko expressed spiritual intentions for his art. Duncan Phillips apparently responded to this when designing the Rothko room for his collection; similarly, the de Menils sensed this quality in the Seagram murals. As Peter Selz has written about those paintings:

> Like much of Rothko's work they really seem to ask for a place apart, a kind of sanctuary where they may perform what is essentially a sacramental function. . . . Perhaps, like medieval altarpieces, [they] can properly be seen only in an ambiance created in total keeping with their mood.[55]

Reviewing Rothko's one-person exhibition at The Museum of Modern Art, Robert Goldwater found, "the most successful arrangement is the small chapel-like room [in which three of the Seagram paintings were hung]. . . . It is significant that at the entrance to this room one pauses, hesitating to enter. Its space seems both occupied and empty."[56]

Responses of this nature, along with the initial visits by the de Menils while the St. Thomas chapel was being discussed, must have contributed to Rothko's evolving ideas about a religious space instead of the secular environment planned for the Seagram paintings or the one-man museum he had talked about previously. The

22. Philip Johnson, Boissonnas House, New Canaan, Connecticut, 1956

painter and writer Ethel Schwabacher recalled that when she visited Rothko's studio in 1962 and commented that some day a museum should be built for his œuvre, Rothko replied, "No. A chapel."[57] This remark should not be interpreted as a desire to paint religious subjects; rather, Rothko may have meant that he found the contemplative environment, the respectful silence of a chapel, to be an appropriate context for his paintings.

While Rothko had not painted explicitly narrative subjects with religious overtones since the early 1940s, his published and private statements often alluded to the religious or spiritual qualities of his work. We have already noted his claim that people who wept upon seeing his paintings were "having the same religious experience I had when I painted them."[58] Rothko "readily agreed [with Katharine Kuh] that most of his paintings, if not strictly religious, were related to realms of the spirit and conceived as contemplative experiences."[59] Seeing the ancient Greek temples at Paestum for the first time in 1959, he remarked, "I have been painting Greek temples all my life without knowing it"; and a few days later he was struck by the affinity of his work with the murals in the Villa of the Mysteries in Pompeii —"the same feeling, the same broad expanses of somber color."[60] To his friends the Scharfs, he remarked, "*All* good painting is a spiritual experience."[61]

Nevertheless, Rothko always denied absolutely that his paintings had any specific religious content—an issue that arose on more than one occasion while he was working on the chapel commission. Knowing that the paintings were destined for a Catholic chapel, visitors to his studio who were not familiar with Rothko's feelings and intentions regarding the commission might ask how the murals related to Christian themes. His assistant during those years recalls, "He *hated* that kind of talk."[62]

From the late 1940s, Rothko's paintings become devoid of subject matter, religious or otherwise, yet they are charged with meaning. Everyone who responds to his paintings agrees on this. The controversy begins, however, as soon as one tries to define their meaning.[63] Rothko once declared, "A painting doesn't need anybody to explain what it is about. If it is any good, it speaks for itself. . ."[64] Rothko stated that he wanted his paintings to be tragic statements of the utmost poignancy; when he invoked religious feelings in speaking of them, we may understand that as a metaphor for the intensity and depth of feeling that he intended.[65] We also know from his statements that he wanted his paintings to transcend specific associations, which he termed "obstacles between the painter and the idea, and between the idea and the observer," such as "memory, history, or geometry."[66] Instead, he sought to express basic human emotions common to people of all religions, in works which may be said to appeal to a universality of experience.

Notes

34. Rothko gave the first of the nine paintings to the Tate in 1968, the rest in 1969; they are all thought to come from the second and third Seagram series (Alley, 1981, p. 660; see also the exhibition catalogue *Mark Rothko 1903–1970,* Tate Gallery, 1987). As was his wont, he "planned the arrangement himself with the aid of a mock-up of the space they were to occupy and even cut a sample of the wall colour from the studio. However, by a sad irony the pictures arrived in London on the very day of his death, and he was never able to see them in position." (Alley, 1981, p. 660). Among the other pictures painted for the Four Seasons, several came with the Rothko bequest to the National Gallery of Art, Washington, D.C.

35. Eliza Rathbone, Curator at the Phillips Collection, kindly searched the records there and supplied the information presented below.

36. According to a copy of the exhibition announcement (Phillips Collection), the exhibitions of January 6–February 26, 1957 also included collages by Kurt Schwitters on the second floor of the Phillips Collection, and paintings by Bradley Walker Tomlin, Mark Rothko and Kenzo Okada in the print rooms. In planning the show in 1956, Phillips stated his intention to hang the Rothko paintings separately in their own room (letter from Duncan Phillips to Sidney Janis, October 26, 1956 [Phillips Collection]). The 1960 exhibition was a one-person exhibition.

37. *Green and Maroon* (1953) and an earlier painting entitled *Mauve Intersection,* both purchased in 1957, were included in the exhibition of May 3–31, 1960, along with four others taken on loan. *Green and Tangerine on Red* (1956), and *Orange and Red on Red* (1957) were acquired in 1960, *Ochre and Red on Red* (1954) in 1964. All but *Mauve Intersection* are in the Phillips Collection today.

38. Arthur Hall Smith, January 12, 1987 (personal communication).

39. Smith, 1987 (personal communication).

40. Katharine Kuh, 1981 (interview), for example, and Peter Selz, 1986 (personal communication).

41. Peter Selz, November 1986 (personal communication).

42. Wilder Green, November 1986 (personal communication).

43. According to Clearwater (1984, p. 62, n. 61) the instructions are still in the possession of the Whitechapel Gallery, with a copy preserved in The Museum of Modern Art.

44. Ashton (1983, pp. 158–161) gives the full story of the commission. While the present study was in press, the Center for Conservation and Technical Studies of the Harvard University Art Museums produced an exhibition and a publication, *Mark Rothko's Harvard Murals* (Cohn, 1988), that thoroughly documents the paintings.

45. Suzannah Fabing, October 1986 (personal communication).

46. Wilder Green, November 1986 (personal communication).

47. Dore Ashton, October 1986 (personal communication).

48. According to a report dated March 15, 1971 by Elizabeth Jones, then conservator at the Fogg, and recorded by Dana L. Cranmer on April 30, 1982 for the Rothko Foundation, Rothko used isolating layers of egg white between layers of oil paint. He also employed pigments that were not colorfast, with the result that by 1971 the paintings had changed from their original crimson to a muted purple (Rothko Foundation documentation, National Gallery of Art, Washington, D.C.).

49. See correspondence between Suzannah Doeringer (Fabing), Asst. Director of the Fogg, and Donald M. Blinken, President of the Rothko Foundation in July 1979 (Rothko Foundation documentation, National Gallery of Art, Washington, D.C.).

50. For more information on Jermayne MacAgy's career in Houston, see Beauchamp, 1983, pp. 16, 21–23, and *Jermayne MacAgy. A Life Illustrated by an Exhibition* (1968–1969).

51. Alfred Frankenstein, *San Francisco Chronicle,* September 23, 1957, quoted in the catalogue of the exhibition *Jermayne MacAgy. A Life Illustrated by an Exhibition* (1968–1969), p. 22.

52. Dominique de Menil, 1979 (conversation with the author).

53. Dominique de Menil, entry made in her 1964 diary, on the page for April 17.

54. Dillenberger, 1969, p. 17.

55. Selz, introductory essay in the catalogue of the Rothko exhibition, 1961, p. 14.

56. Goldwater, 1961, p. 45.

57. Recounted by Ethel Schwabacher, 1981 (conversation with the author).

58. Rodman, 1975, pp. 93–94.

59. Kuh, 1981 (interview), from the manuscript of her memoirs about Rothko.

60. Quoted in Fischer, 1970, p. 22.

61. William and Sally Scharf, June 24, 1982 (interview).

62. Edwards, 1977 (interview).

63. Brian O'Doherty (1970, p. 30) lamented, "Rothko's art utters a single word insistently. But everyone hears it differently. The community functions perfectly until someone tries to describe the word."

64. Fischer, 1970, p. 20.

65. Lee Seldes reports that Rothko also used a Christian analogy when speaking to Nathan Pusey about the Harvard murals (*The Legacy of Mark Rothko* [New York, 1978], p. 51).

66. *15 Americans,* p. 18.

The Making of the Chapel

The Making of the Chapel:
The Plan and the Paintings

Mark Rothko had already been working for several months on the chapel project when the contract between the artist and the University of St. Thomas was signed February 13, 1965. In it Rothko agreed:

> . . . to make a sufficient number of paintings to illumine adequately the interior of the new chapel at the University of St. Thomas which is being designed by Mr. Philip Johnson. Since it is an octagon shape with an apse, it seems at the present moment that there will be ten units—one to each of the sides and three for the apse. This, of course, may be altered in the course of the work. Upon completion of the paintings, I will, together with Mr. Johnson, supervise their installation and lighting. The completion of these paintings will take about 24 months from January 1, 1965. [67]

The University agreed to pay a fee of $250,000 for the paintings, plus out-of-pocket expenses including the rent of the carriage house at 153 E. 69th St. that Rothko had taken as a studio. That amount would be offered as a gift to the university by John and Dominique de Menil. Funds for building the chapel were given by the de Menils and other contributors. As the architect of the St. Thomas campus, Philip Johnson had begun consulting with Rothko as soon as the latter had accepted the commission.

In Rothko's two previous series—the murals for the Seagram Building, and those for Harvard—he had made paintings for spaces which were already designed. [68] With the Houston chapel, for the first time he had a role in determining the form and dimensions of

the architecture, in shaping the environment that was to house his works. Rothko participated actively in designing the chapel interior, and only after the specifications of the plan and interior walls were decided upon did he begin work on the paintings *(fig. 23)*.

23. Rothko in his 69th St. studio during construction of chapel mock-up, New York, 1964

The Plan

On July 7, 1964, Dore Ashton visited the Rothkos at the house they had rented on Long Island.[69] After lunch she went with Rothko to the beach, and he told her about the commission he had received from the de Menils. Although he had not begun formally to work on the paintings, Rothko had already given thought to the setting. He declared that he wanted the chapel to be an octagon.

Reflecting on this idea of the octagon, Dominique de Menil believes that Rothko was motivated by purely artistic considerations. Afraid that the octagonal shape might be rejected, he sought to justify it by looking for precedents. He went as far as pretending to her that he had spoken to Meyer Shapiro and learned from him that indeed such central plans had been used in early Christian times.

While historical associations may have been meaningful to Rothko, we may assume that his primary criterion was the way the plan would serve his murals. Rothko's choice of the octagon was well suited to frontality and symmetry, both of which are salient characteristics of the paintings. Because the octagon is a radially symmetric plan, from the center of the space the spectator can view each painting squarely, from an equal distance. The walls of the octagon meet at a gentle obtuse angle, permitting a smooth transition from one painting to another and virtually encircling the viewer.

Within the symmetry of the octagonal space, Rothko created patterns of internal symmetry. For instance, the black-form triptychs that mirror each other on the east and west walls give a somber, lateral symmetry. On the other hand, the four plum-colored canvases that hang individually on the short, off-compass-point walls lend a radial symmetry to the arrangement. At the same time, they flank the paintings contained on the long walls, making symmetrical groupings that span three walls.

Rothko called his paintings "voices in an opera," and we shall see the long process he went through to achieve the effect that he wanted.[70] The octagonal plan would help achieve this, setting the works in diagonal, lateral, or oblique relation across the space to one another, allowing Rothko's "voices" to be heard either individually or combined, in counterpoint or unison.

Dore Ashton's notes confirm that Rothko had set his mind on an octagonal plan. Rather than proposing the octagon immediately, however, he appears to have let the plan emerge from a series of

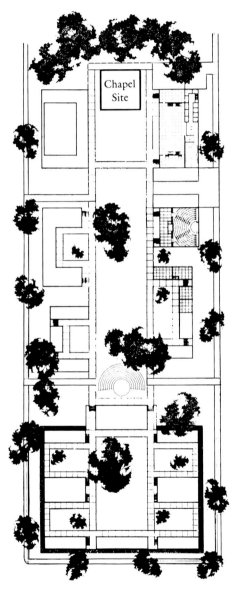

24. Philip Johnson, master plan, University of St. Thomas, 1957 (as published, 1959).

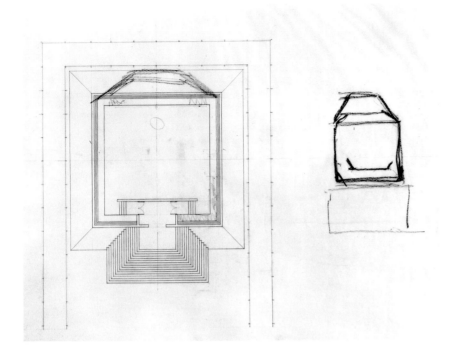

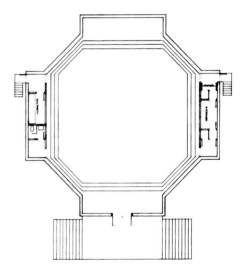

25. Philip Johnson, square plan, apse drawn in by Rothko, 1964

26. Philip Johnson, octagonal plan, 1964

discussions with Philip Johnson, for whom the chapel architecture was part of the master plan he had devised for the university.[71] The only record of these discussions is a group of architectural drawings from the Rothko estate; dates on corresponding plans from Johnson's archive show these meetings to have taken place in October of 1964.[72] The drawings that remained in Rothko's possession are covered with pencil and chalk corrections showing how the plan evolved, step by step, from the square proposed by Philip Johnson on the master plan *(fig. 24)*, to a square with an apse *(fig. 25)*, and finally to the octagon itself *(fig. 26)*.

The form and dimensions of the chapel interior were settled upon by Johnson and Rothko in fall 1964. It was to be an octagonal ground plan with a rectilinear apse and a recessed floor. At this early stage, perhaps before putting brush to canvas, Rothko continued to consider the paintings in terms of their setting. We have evidence of this in two other architectural drawings amended in Rothko's hand. In one *(fig. 27)*, on the left side of an early elevation, Rothko drew a view of the walls with paintings in place. In the other, a cross-section, a few pencil lines indicate where Rothko imagined the participants in the mass to be, and how they would perceive his paintings *(fig. 28)*. At the far right, three steps descend from the apse to the recessed floor; to the left is the altar with the celebrant standing behind it; rough rectangles represent the paintings on the

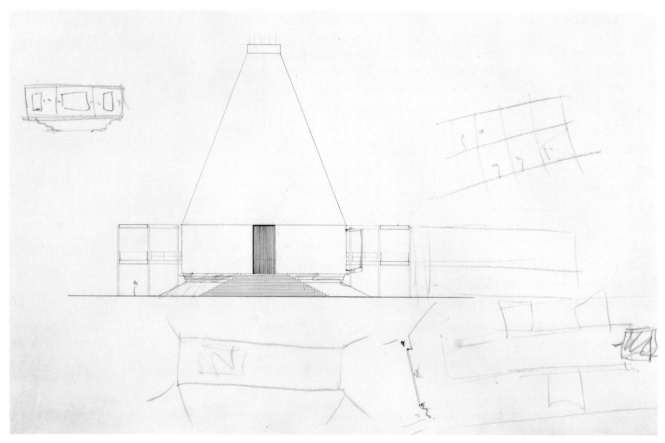

walls, and a few soft lines above trace the flow of light through
the oculus down into the space; at the left, three strong horizontal
lines reinforce the lines of the steps under the far wall. Finally,
the head of a congregation member seems to be represented by a
solid black dot nearly in the middle of the space, from which a
ruled line drawn to the topmost point of the apse wall suggests
the participant's line of vision.

As he had done with the Seagram commission, Rothko had a
full-scale mock-up of three of the chapel walls built in his 69th St.
studio. It was completed by December 17, 1964.[73] For the duration
of the project he would work on those walls. Working with the
actual space was an essential part of Rothko's procedure: although
he would avail himself of architect's models to study arrangements
of the chapel paintings, or test compositional ideas in small paper
studies as he had done with the Harvard and Seagram murals, all
the real decisions would be made at full scale.

Scale and proportion were the heart of the matter. Dore Ashton wrote of the early stages of work on the chapel murals,

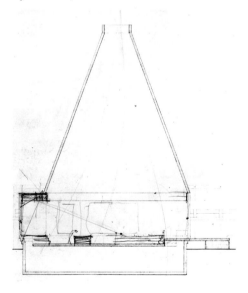

There were times when the vast stretchers—wooden carriers without their canvas—were leaned against the walls and contemplated for days. Times when the entire canvas on one of those stretchers had to be given up because the scale was not quite right. For months he measured and measured with his eye. [74]

The architectural mock-up was crucial to the "measuring" process mentioned, a process that continued until the end. The exact size of each canvas to the fraction of an inch, the relationship within a canvas of the form to the ground, the relationship of each painting to the others—in short, every decision, each fine calibration of the components of the ensemble was made precisely in relation to the walls where the paintings would hang. As we shall see, the actual painting, even of these large works, involved relatively little time; but before and after each flurry of painterly activity, Rothko would spend untold hours contemplating the paintings in their architectural setting, measuring with the eye and with the mind.

The Paintings

Most of what we know about the making of the paintings for the Rothko Chapel we owe to the three men who assisted Rothko during those years: William Scharf, Roy Edwards, and Ray Kelly. Rothko painted alone. Moreover, he was secretive about his technique, and his assistants were not supposed to watch him when he worked; all the materials he used would be put away when visitors came.[75] Scharf worked with him from summer 1964 to fall 1965; Edwards and Kelly came on in December 1965 and January 1966 respectively, with the latter staying on until after the murals were completed in spring 1967. Their recollections of collaborating with Rothko include many details, technical or otherwise, concerning the making of the paintings. From the information provided by these three men, we may construct a hypothetical sequence of events and activities in the making of the paintings for the Rothko Chapel.[76]

29. Rothko's 69th St. studio with chapel paintings on pulley system, 1965

William Scharf, a painter himself and a friend of Rothko since the early 1950s, had occasionally helped out in his studio over the years, whenever the older artist needed some assistance.[77] In the summer of 1964 when the Rothko family went to Amagansett, Scharf and his wife Sally maintained their 95th St. house. Rothko had just rented the 69th St. studio, and during his absence Scharf oversaw its installation, which consisted mainly of building storage racks for the artist's paintings. Although Rothko may have already begun some sketches or first ideas for the chapel commission while he was away, and we know from Dore Ashton that he had been thinking about the ground plan, we have no evidence that work began in earnest until his return in fall 1964.

The year that Scharf worked with Rothko, from fall 1964 to fall 1965, seems to constitute a first phase in the making of the chapel paintings. Because of the nature of the commission, Rothko had estimated that he would need two years to complete it. Scharf recalls that first year as one of experiments, "of trial and error."

After Rothko returned from vacation, Scharf put together stretchers ordered from Lou Sgroi, while the mock-up walls were being built. When the proper stretcher sizes had been chosen, Scharf stretched as many as a dozen of them with unprimed cotton duck. Scharf came regularly to assist Rothko in the studio, because the individual canvases for the environment were so large that two men were needed to move them. (Once they were hung on the mock-up walls, Rothko devised an elaborate system of pulleys by which he could adjust their height by himself [*fig. 29*].) In addition to the deliberation about the proportions of the stretchers described by Ashton, Scharf remembers that there was extensive experimentation with technique. Rothko worked with a thin, difficult medium—dry pigments dissolved in heated rabbitskin glue—and once he had decided on the kind of surface he wanted, a way had to be found of obtaining it on the unusually large canvases. To achieve a uniform texture over such vast areas called for a speed of application beyond the power of one person, so Scharf helped Rothko apply the paint as well. He recounts the awkward way they first went about this: a painting was hung vertically on a wall of the mock-up; either Scharf or Rothko stood on a ladder and quickly brushed the thin paint onto the top of the canvas while the other man did the same standing below, trying not to get entangled in the ladder. According to Scharf, all the colors used in these first works were dark: brick reds, deep reds, black mauves. He remembers that Rothko was pleased when Scharf took a painted canvas

and scrubbed it down, allowing it to be used again.

By fall 1965, when Scharf stopped assisting Rothko on the chapel paintings, there were many canvases in the studio that had been worked on. Two of these document an interesting but eventually abandoned stage in Rothko's ideas.[78] They are very long, low paintings, each measuring about 21 × 179 in.; one *(fig. 30)* is black on red, the other *(fig. 31)* is black on maroon. Each painting has three loosely-brushed forms: two long rectangles flanking a central form with one side hollowed out in a rounded niche. According to Scharf, Rothko had already planned to group the murals into one or more triptychs; these long, low paintings were intended to hang directly beneath the triptychs, in much the same manner as predellae do on Renaissance altarpieces. Now in The Menil Collection, these two paintings are our only remaining full-scale evidence of this design.[79]

The period from fall 1965 until the murals were completed in spring 1967 may be considered the second phase of work, marked by major changes in Rothko's technique and working method. For instance, it marks his first use of a taped edge, a formal device employed in the work of Rothko's younger contemporaries. Also for the first time he adopted an approach employed by many younger artists during the 1960s of distancing himself from the process, entrusting the physical execution of the chapel paintings to his assistants. Rothko had worked with an assistant before—on the Seagram commission, for instance, when he was younger and more physically able to work on an environmental scale. While he worked with Scharf in 1964–1965, however, the magnitude of the chapel commission became apparent, both in terms of the number of paintings and their enormous size. Rothko's health was not good, and able-bodied help was in order. After Scharf left, Rothko

30. Mark Rothko
Untitled (Est. no. 6027.59S), n.d.
Dry pigments, polymer, rabbitskin glue
    and egg/oil emulsion on canvas
21 × 178⅝ in.
The Menil Collection, Houston

31. Mark Rothko
Untitled (Est. no. 6028.59S), n.d.
Dry pigments, polymer, rabbitskin glue
    and egg/oil emulsion on canvas
21⅛ × 181⅞ in.
The Menil Collection, Houston

hired two young art students to assist him: Roy Edwards and Ray Kelly. He would supervise them scrupulously, but he would give them the lion's share to do in applying the paint to canvas.

As we view the Rothko Chapel and its seemingly perfect balance of interlocking elements—seven canvases with hard-edged black rectangles on maroon ground, and seven plum-colored tonal paintings—it is important to note that both were unprecedented in Rothko's œuvre. Just as with the two previous mural series, Rothko responded to the challenge of the chapel commission by making changes in his work—innovations that would in turn renew the rest of his œuvre. In all the mural series, he diverged from his customary soft-edged rectangles floating against a background. The paintings for the Seagram Building and for Harvard have open, loosely-brushed rectangular forms. For the chapel, on the other hand, he took his usual approach to two opposite extremes: in some of the paintings he eliminated form altogether, leaving only a thin, evanescent ground; in others he consolidated form into a single, large rectangle whose taped, hard-edged limits are as absolute as its impenetrable blackness.

Many factors were doubtless involved in Rothko's decision to abandon his distinctively brushed forms in favor of the hard, mechanical, taped edge. Some of his friends have remarked that Rothko was thinking about Ad Reinhardt's virtually monochromatic hard-edged paintings of this time, and that these were an influence on him.[80] In spring 1964 before beginning the chapel paintings, Rothko had made some canvases with a single dark, hard-edged form on a dark plum ground.[81] It seems likely, too, that an interest in architecture played a role in Rothko's opting for hard-edged forms. Herbert Ferber recalls that Rothko was absorbed with some illustrations in a book on Florentine Renaissance architecture that Philip Johnson had lent him: in the strong Italian light, the windows that cut into the massive walls of those buildings were like black rectangles against the lighter gray stone walls.[82] The interior architecture of the chapel itself also would have stimulated Rothko as he worked daily in the mock-up in his studio. Philip Johnson remembers that Rothko was very enthusiastic about the chapel doorways, rectangles cut into the wall surface.[83]

Rothko had made substantial progress in developing his ideas during the first year's experiments, now he was ready to carry them out. Roy Edwards came to work in Rothko's studio late in 1965, recommended to Rothko as an assistant by Theodoros Stamos, Edwards' teacher at the Art Students League. Ray Kelly, another of

32. Mark Rothko in his studio, New York, ca. 1964

Stamos' students and Edwards' roommate at that time, was hired in January 1966. Edwards recalls,

> My first impression of Rothko was that he was something of a Bavarian clockmaker—very careful and slow and precise. All his movements were like thought out before hand. He seemed to know exactly where he was at. We got into the work right away. [84] *(fig. 32)*

Edwards' first assignment was to help Rothko study the effect of the ensemble of paintings in the space. Following Rothko's instructions, he made a number of small cardboard rectangles painted in different colors, including plum and black. [85] These they tested in the architect's model of the chapel interior that had been provided by Philip Johnson's office. This model, which Rothko kept, still bears the traces of these experiments in the bits of colored paper glued to the walls *(fig. 33)*. [86]

To prepare new canvases, huge seamless pieces of unprimed cotton duck were stretched onto the Lou Sgroi stretchers. [87] Edwards and Rothko laid out the stretchers on large tabletops supported by sawhorses, then rolled the canvas out over them, cut, and stretched it. They would spend one day stretching and the next day or two correcting a canvas, which had been wet down with sponge mops so it would dry tightly on its support. If there was the slightest imperfection in the canvas weave, Rothko would throw away the entire piece of material. These preparations went on for about a month, until several canvases were ready to be painted.

All the paintings made for the chapel have the same two primary coats. The first layer consists of dry pigments, alizarin crimson and an ultramarine blue, mixed in hot rabbitskin glue. [88] Rothko chose the colors, then supervised as his assistants did the laborious mixing, boiling and stirring the medium to which the pigments had been added, until it was very watery and thin. To cover such large unprimed surfaces required many buckets of paint, each one mixed separately; the variations we see today in the plum-colored paintings are due to the slightly varying proportions of these different mixtures. When a batch of paint was ready, it was applied with the paintings lying on their side. [89] Instead of hanging the oversize canvases vertically as he had done when working with Scharf, Rothko had them placed on their side against a wall. Then while Rothko directed their work, the two assistants Edwards and Kelly applied the paint using housepainter's brushes 4 to 6 inches wide, working rapidly from opposite ends of the canvas toward the mid-

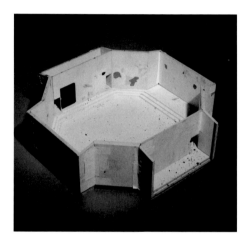

33. Philip Johnson, scale model of chapel, 1965
5⅜ × 16½ × 16½ in.
The Menil Collection, Houston

34. Mark Rothko
Untitled (study for chapel), ca. 1965
Pencil on construction paper
9 × 12 in.
The Menil Collection, Houston

35. Mark Rothko
Untitled (study for chapel), ca. 1965
Pencil on construction paper
6½ × 10⅜ in.
The Menil Collection, Houston

dle. Edwards and Kelly brushed the paint on as Rothko instructed: in horizontal strokes, working from top to bottom and across, to give a vertical direction to the strokes when the paintings were placed upright. The second coat has the same pigments with the addition of bone-black dry pigment to make the color darker, but here the medium was a synthetic polymer.[90] This mixture was applied in the same way as the first. These two coats are all there

36. Mark Rothko
Untitled (study for chapel), ca. 1965
Pencil on construction paper
6¾ × 9¾ in.
The Menil Collection, Houston

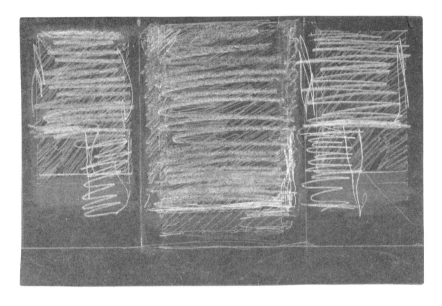

37. Mark Rothko
Untitled (study for chapel), ca. 1965
Pencil on construction paper
6½ × 10½ in.
The Menil Collection, Houston

is on the plum-colored paintings—those in the apse triptych and on the off-compass-point walls of the chapel. The same two coats became the ground for the black forms that would be applied to the remaining paintings.[91]

Rothko gave great deliberation and went through a long process of trial and error to determine the size and shape of the black rectangles for these paintings. Small graphite studies on paper *(figs. 34–38)* were part of that process. These all involve the black-form paintings arranged as triptychs, and they may date to mid-1965, before Rothko gave up the idea of including predella-like paintings. A comparison of these studies with the stages of work on the paintings themselves (now clearly visible in pentimenti) indicates that the proportions of the black forms in each painting that comprises the triptychs were developed as a whole, each element in relation to the others.

The graphite studies show some alternatives considered by Rothko for the relationship of the black rectangle in the central panel to those in the side panels. Should the rectangles be of the same height *(fig. 34)*? Should they all be the same width proportionate to the width of the canvas *(fig. 35)*, or should those on the side be shorter and narrower *(fig. 36)*? In one drawing, Rothko even experimented with an irregular shape for the forms in the side panels *(fig. 37)*.

The real study and decision-making, however, went on at full scale. Rothko had his assistants take a plum-colored canvas, mark off the area he chose with masking tape, and blacken that part of the canvas with charcoal. Then they would leave him to study this full-scale sketch against the architecture of the mock-up, and in relation to other canvases. During these periods of reflection, Edwards remembers,

> I would come in, you know, and maybe clean the studio, and he'd be inside listening to Mozart and looking at the paintings. When he'd reach a decision to make a change in the picture— it would be like to reduce the dimensions of the borders, to increase the black area maybe a half-inch or more. . . even a quarter-inch. I would retape the whole black form a quarter-inch and put in charcoal to expand it. . . . This went on for about a month, altering the interior dimensions, in and out. I'd reduce the black form by just brushing the charcoal away, or I'd make it larger. And when he finally made a decision, a fresh canvas was brought out—one that was already primed. The dimensions were put down with masking tape.[92]

Then the canvas would be turned on its side and leaned against the wall for the application of the black paint. According to Edwards, Rothko painted all the black forms himself.[93] This differs from Kelly's recollection that Rothko painted the form on the first four or five canvases, but then supervised the work of the two assistants as they painted the others.[94] According to Kelly, the medium they used was an egg-oil emulsion, consisting of whole egg, oil paint, dammar resin, and turpentine.[95] Deciding that the background plum color was too light relative to the looming black forms, Rothko had another coat of red, blue, and black pigments in a polymer medium applied, to darken the color of the borders to maroon.

Pentimenti, or traces of successive layers of black paint that can be seen beneath the final coat, show us today that the artist's process of reflection and revision continued in both triptychs even after the black form was set in paint. These pentimenti are more apparent now than when the paintings were first made, but Rothko saw them even then, and accepted them as evidence of the process.[96] They reveal that the black rectangles were progressively expanded to the point of nearly filling the field, leaving the ground as a narrow border.

Pentimenti in the central canvas of the eastern triptych show that although still centered, the black rectangle was widened twice. In the side panels, pentimenti show changes revealing that Rothko first placed the rectangular forms strongly off-center, leaving a wide border at the outside edge and a narrower one at the inside edge. To imagine the effect of this design, it is important to remember that the triptych's three canvases were originally intended to be hung in a straight horizontal alignment; in the final scheme of the chapel, however, Rothko raised the central canvas higher than the two flanking ones. The graphite studies we have already seen (*figs. 34–37*) show that if the three parts are aligned, the triptych can be read either as three contiguous vertical canvases or as a single horizontal field with three rectangular forms. None of the surviving studies corresponds precisely to any of the pentimenti in the eastern triptych. Nevertheless, one of the graphite studies (*fig. 38*) gives an idea of how the narrow inside border of the side panel would have combined with the identically-colored adjacent border of the center canvas to balance the broad border of the outer edge. In this first stage, the rectangles in the side panels were not only much narrower and placed off-center, they were also shorter than the central black rectangle, at both top and bottom. In subsequent stages—seen still in the pentimenti—Rothko extended the side rectangles above and below, and on their edges, thus making these rectangles the same height as the central rectangle, and also wider and nearer to the center of their respective canvases.

The fact that this eastern triptych has many more pentimenti than the corresponding western one suggests that Rothko made it first. The western triptych, after the lessons learned on the first, bears fewer traces of deliberation and change; there the pentimenti show that the black rectangles were first smaller, then enlarged to their present size. This triptych is not a mere duplication of the

38. Mark Rothko
Untitled (study for chapel), ca. 1965
Pencil on construction paper
6¾ × 9¾ in.
The Menil Collection, Houston

first, however. Rothko approached these as three fresh paintings. The pentimenti differ from one triptych to the next, and the final dimensions of the black forms in the western triptych are also slightly different from those in the eastern triptych.

Apart from the six canvases comprising the eastern and western triptychs, five other individual black-form paintings were completed for the chapel. Of these, Rothko finally placed only one in the ensemble: it hangs alone on the south wall, opposite the apse. The other four black-form paintings—now in The Menil Collection—were sent into storage by Rothko along with the others, for later shipment to Houston (fig. 39). As he had done for the Harvard and Seagram murals, Rothko painted several more canvases than necessary for the chapel walls.[97] What place the extra paintings might finally have had in the scheme is uncertain; Rothko had intended to oversee the chapel installation personally, and he included these four additional black-form paintings in the shipment to Houston, leaving possible alternatives open. But the murals were hung in the chapel after Rothko's death, and the present installation reflects the last one he recorded before sending them all into storage.[98]

As each painting was finished Rothko brought it into relationship with the others, experimenting with different arrangements of the ensemble. Since the full-scale mock-up of the chapel in Rothko's studio included only three of the eight walls, to help envision the effect of the entire ensemble he kept a working scale model of the interior. This model was open at the bottom, and large enough that

39. Mark Rothko
Untitled (additional painting from
    chapel series), 1965
Dry pigments, polymer, rabbitskin glue
    and egg/oil emulsion on canvas
177 in. × 96¼ in.
The Menil Collection, Houston

one could put one's head inside it and approximate the experience of standing within the chapel space *(fig. 40)*;[99] Dore Ashton recalls it as being in the studio antechamber.[100]

Rothko gave close attention to the exact height and placement of each painting on each wall, which he could calculate precisely since the chapel walls were to be built to exactly the same dimensions as those in his studio mock-up. To move the paintings up and down on the walls, he used the system of ropes and pulleys already mentioned. These experiments with placement resulted in further alterations to the paintings. For instance, Rothko decided to shorten by two and a half inches the height of the two plum-colored canvases that hang to the right and the left of the apse triptych, on the grounds that this made for a better optical relationship between them.[101] This fine-tuning process went on for months.[102]

In the chapel paintings, Rothko was striving for "a maximum of poignancy," but also for "precision."[103] His large, dark paintings would speak more softly, convey their message more slowly, than any he had ever made; yet he wanted them to speak eloquently, and their message to be felt intensely. Rothko brought all of his dramatic and musical sensibilities into play as he orchestrated these voices; and he tirelessly rehearsed the arrangement in all its possible modifications, sometimes in the presence of visitors, usually just one or two at a time.

Rothko observed the response of these visitors and asked for their suggestions, some of which he followed. Late in 1966, for instance, on a friend's advice, he decided to raise the central panel of each of the two black-form triptychs to a higher position than the side panels.[104] Visitors to the studio then saw how he had mounted the three panels of the triptych on easels that could be raised and lowered independently of one another. Rothko would adjust the height of the central panel relative to the side ones, trying several different positions for them, and asking which they thought was best.[105] It is this raised position of the central panel as he finally determined it which we see now.

Rothko's last configuration of the chapel paintings is comprised of eight separate, essential units *(fig. 41)*. On the north wall (the apse) is a triptych, comprised of three abutted canvases; on the east and west walls are similar triptychs, also with three abutted canvases each; on the south wall is a single narrower vertical painting; and completing the octagon plan are four broad single paintings, one on each of the diagonal walls. In the literature about

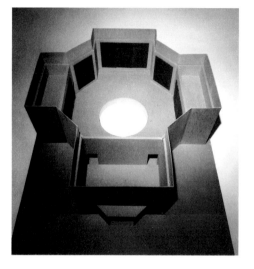

40. Philip Johnson, scale model of chapel, ca. 1965
12¾ × 37¼ × 40½ in.
The Menil Collection, Houston

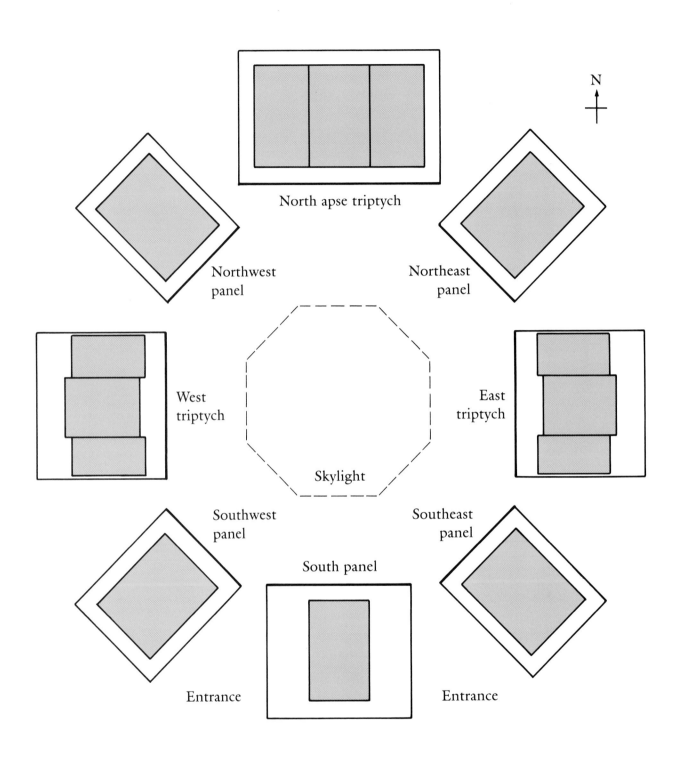

North apse triptych

Northwest panel

Northeast panel

N

West triptych

East triptych

Skylight

Southwest panel

Southeast panel

South panel

Entrance

Entrance

41. Rothko Chapel, diagrammatic plan –
final arrangement of paintings

the chapel, the incidental fact that these eight units can theoretically be separated into fourteen individual canvases has sometimes given rise to a misapprehended notion of a correspondence with the fourteen Stations of the Cross.[106]

There is no evidence to suggest that Rothko intended any allusion to the Stations of the Cross in these paintings. Early in the project, even before the chapel was built, when it was still planned to function as a Catholic chapel at the University of St. Thomas, the St. Thomas fathers raised the issue of the liturgical requirement for symbols of the Stations of the Cross. Rothko had agreed in principle to any necessary cult object, provided no other modern work of art would be placed in the chapel, but he balked completely at the idea of including symbols of the Stations of the Cross. He conceded that if it were absolutely necessary, markers might be placed on the outside walls.[107] This compromise, however, was never necessary, since by the time of its dedication the chapel had become an ecumenical structure.

In speaking about the chapel murals, the only religious comment Rothko ever made to Dominique de Menil was to mention the emotions he experienced in the Byzantine basilica church of S. Maria Assunta at Torcello.[108] He had been struck with awe by the mosaic of the Last Judgment at the entrance (fig. 43), then this ominous feeling had been superseded by the vision of the Madonna and Child on a golden background in the apse (fig. 44). He said he had sought to create, between the chapel's entrance and its apse, the same tension he had felt at Torcello—that between doom and promise.

Mark Rothko telephoned John de Menil in the middle of April 1967 to tell him that the murals were finished (Plates I–IV).[109] The paintings remained in his studio for another few weeks; then since construction of the chapel had not yet been begun, it was decided to free Rothko's studio by taking them to storage. On June 6, 1967, Dominique de Menil came to the 69th St. studio, accompanied by her assistant Helen Winkler and the architect Howard Barnstone. Paintings were hanging on the three mock-up walls, exactly as Rothko wanted them to hang in the chapel. For the five remaining walls, Rothko had written out, to the fraction of an inch, the exact placement he wanted, and these dimensions were conveyed directly by telephone from Rothko's studio to Barnstone's office in Houston where they were recorded on a drawing (fig. 42).[110] A note on that drawing shows the degree of Rothko's care over fine details, for on June 7, the very next day, he ordered further slight

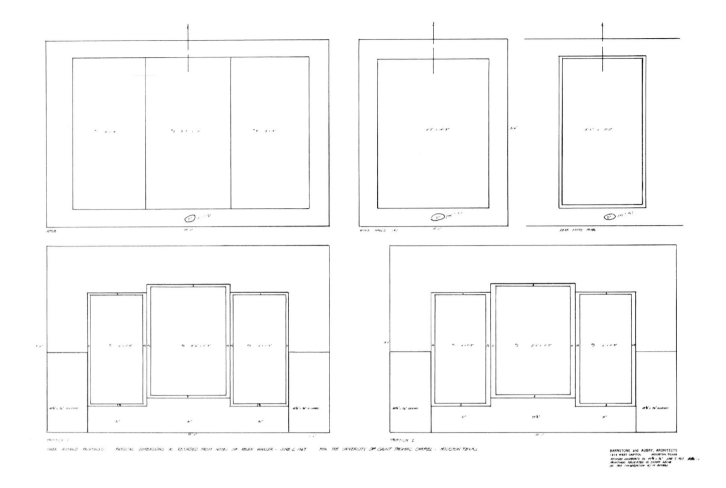

adjustments to the size of the doorways and the position of the paintings. Rothko's continuing involvement with the chapel murals even after they had left the studio, and his customary concern with the installation of his paintings, make it clear that he intended to participate actively in the hanging in Houston. But that was not to be.

In the spring of 1968, Rothko suffered an aneurysm of the heart; unable to work, he became irritable. Excessive drink and depression had long been a part of Rothko's life, but in his illness their effects grew more pronounced than before. He quarrelled with those whom he loved, broke off relations with old friends; eventually he separated from his wife and went to live in the 69th St. studio. When he began to recover and was again able to paint, at first he could only work on small paintings on paper. As his health improved, he undertook larger-scale paintings on paper, and mended fences with friends. In 1969 he received an honorary doctorate from Yale University, the school he had attended for a while as an

42. Barnstone and Aubry, drawing recording Rothko's instructions for placement of the chapel paintings, 1967

43. *The Last Judgement* (details)
Santa Maria Assunta, Torcello, Italy, 1190

44. *Madonna and Child* (detail)
Santa Maria Assunta, Torcello, Italy, 1190

undergraduate. He was finally strong enough to paint on canvas once more, and that year he donated some of the Seagram murals to The Tate Gallery in London, where they were to be permanently housed.[111] Early in 1970, he received a clean bill of health from his doctor. Ground had just been broken for the Rothko Chapel, and final details were being fixed with the artist's close consultation. He was pleased with all of this, and when the architect Eugene Aubry visited him in early February, talked of driving to Texas for the chapel's opening.[112] But in the early hours of February 25, Mark Rothko took his own life.

Plate I   Mark Rothko
Untitled (South wall painting), 1964–67
Dry pigments, polymer, rabbitskin glue
   and egg/oil emulsion on canvas
180 × 105 in.
Rothko Chapel, Houston

Plate II   Mark Rothko
            Untitled (East wall triptych), 1964–67
            Dry pigments, polymer, rabbitskin glue
               and egg/oil emulsion on canvas
            134⅞ × 245¾ in.
            Rothko Chapel, Houston

Plate III   Mark Rothko
             Untitled (Northwest wall painting), 1964–67
             Dry pigments, polymer, rabbitskin glue
                and egg/oil emulsion on canvas
             177½ × 135 in.
             Rothko Chapel, Houston

Plate IV   Mark Rothko
            Untitled (North apse triptych), 1964–67
            Dry pigments, polymer, rabbitskin glue
              and egg/oil emulsion on canvas
            180 × 297 in.
            Rothko Chapel, Houston

Notes

67. Menil Foundation, Houston.

68. For some of the problems that such an assignment involved, see the interview with Dan Rice in *The 1958–59 Murals: Second Series,* 1978, n.p.

69. Ashton, 1971, p. 274, and *idem.,* 1983, p. 126. Ms. Ashton kindly allowed me to consult her dated notes of the meeting to verify this important fact.

70. Robert Motherwell quoted Rothko on "voices in an opera," 1980 (interview); Kuh, 1971, p. 52.

71. Johnson's master plan for the University of St. Thomas was published in *Architectural Record* (September 1959, p. 180).

72. Mr. Johnson kindly donated all of the original drawings relating to the Rothko Chapel to the Menil Foundation, Houston. Prints of these can also be found in Johnson's archive.

73. Letter from Philip Johnson to John de Menil, December 17, 1964 (Menil Foundation).

74. Ashton, 1971, p. 274.

75. Edwards and Pomeroy, 1971, p. 116. Rothko apparently never discussed technique with other artists (Motherwell, 1980 [interview]). One exception was the sculptor Herbert Ferber, who, when he began painting seriously in the late 1950s, asked Rothko about his medium. Rothko told him then that he mixed his colors in egg white, dammar varnish, and linseed oil (Ferber, 1981 [interview]).

76. The information came in correspondence, telephone conversations, and interviews with William Scharf, Roy Edwards, and Ray Kelly conducted by Dominique de Menil, Carol Mancusi-Ungaro, Mary Jane Victor, and/or the author; records of these are kept in The Menil Collection. See also Edwards and Pomeroy, 1971, pp. 109–121, and *The 1958–59 Murals: Second Series,* 1978, n.p.

77. William Scharf provided the following information (June 1982 [interview]).

78. I am very grateful to Bonnie Clearwater for bringing these to my attention.

79. Bonnie Clearwater suggested that predellae also figure in a series of graphite studies (figs. 34–37). She sees the shallow, blank area beneath the triptych in each study as a predella (1984, pp. 50–51).

80. H. Ferber (1981 [interview]), and K. Kuh (1981 [interview]), both recalled Rothko's referring to Reinhardt's paintings.

According to his assistant, Roy Edwards, "Rothko liked to joke about masking tape being the foundation of modern art." (Edwards and Pomeroy, 1971, pp. 114–115).

81. When Robert and Jane Meyerhoff visited Rothko's studio in spring 1964 they saw five such paintings, one of which they purchased ten years later (Sundell, 1980, unpaginated preface by Jane B. Meyerhoff, and illustrated on p. 61).

82. Ferber, 1981 (interview). Ferber remembers that at an early stage Rothko was thinking about arranging the paintings in an architectonic manner inspired by these Renaissance fenestrations.

83. Johnson, 1979 (interview).

84. Edwards and Pomeroy, 1971, p. 111.

85. Edwards, 1977 (interview).

86. The model and two colored cardboard studies are now in The Menil Collection, Houston, but the studies are slightly too large to have been used in the small model. One is a black rectangle glued to a plum ground, while the second represents a plum-colored triptych. The other surviving studies are all drawings on paper, and all of them involve the black-form triptychs. See below.

87. Edwards, 1977 (interview).

88. Edwards, 1977 (interview); Kelly, 1980 (interview).

89. Edwards, 1977 (interview).

90. Kelly, 1980 (interview), and 1983 (personal communication). The identification of these pigments was confirmed by Carol Mancusi-Ungaro, Conservator of The Menil Collection, but the medium has not yet been tested. (See her forthcoming publication on the conservation of the Rothko Chapel paintings.) In contrast, Edwards recalled the mixture included oil paint and turpentine as well as dry pigments, and that the colors were alizarin crimson and black (Edwards and Pomeroy, 1971, p. 113).

91. Some question arises as to the preparation of the black-form painting on the south wall, since the visible plum background is an egg/oil emulsion like the black-form. Priming layers may be comparable to the other paintings, but that remains undetermined at this time.

92. Edwards and Pomeroy, 1971, pp. 114–115.

93. Edwards and Pomeroy, 1971, p. 115.

94. Kelly, 1983 (personal communication), stated that he and Edwards painted the black forms in both triptychs but not in the single canvas on the south wall of the chapel. This last one and the four extras were painted already when he came to work for Rothko, and seem to have been done by Rothko alone.

95. Kelly, 1980 (interview). Note that this is different from the mixture he described to Ferber (see note 60 above): here the egg yolk is included as well as the white. The unexpected use of both parts of the egg, to which Ray Kelly attested, was again borne out by Mancusi-Ungaro's analysis.

96. Edwards, 1977 (interview), notes that Rothko expanded the width of certain paintings, by re-stretching them on slightly wider stretchers, then adding pieces of canvas to their sides and painting the edges to match. Physical examination of the paintings has not thus far confirmed this.

97. William Scharf, 1980 (interview), says that Rothko made extras for all of his commissions. The four extras for the chapel, two measuring 177×96 in. and two $177\text{-}1/2 \times 96$ in., are in The Menil Collection, Houston.

98. See below, note 110.

99. This model is now at The Menil Collection. According to Herbert Ferber, 1981 (personal communication), the idea for using this kind of model came from E. C. Goosen. He had suggested it to Ferber in 1960 as a tool for better measuring the effect of Ferber's environmental sculptures (Goosen, 1981, pp. 104–105).

100. Ashton, 1986 (personal communication).

101. D. de Menil, 1971, p. 251.

102. Kelly, 1983 (personal communication).

103. Kuh, 1971, p. 81; Ashton, 1971, p. 274.

104. Rothko told this to Dominique de Menil in 1966, but he did not identify the person who made the suggestion.

105. This was witnessed by Walter Widrig, a professor of art history at Rice University who then was teaching at the University of St. Thomas. He visited the studio on December 31, 1966 with Dominique de Menil, her son François, and Widrig's colleague Philip Oliver-Smith. Rothko had invited Mrs. de Menil and her guests to the studio to ask their opinion of the new arrangement of the triptych. Widrig recalls that by then Rothko said he had decided which paintings he would hang on all of the walls except the one at the entrance (Walter Widrig, 1982 [personal communication]).

106. For example, Waldman, 1978, p. 68.

107. D. de Menil, 1978 (personal communication).

108. D. de Menil, 1971, p. 251; and personal communication (January 1987).

109. Letter from John de Menil to Mrs. Otto Spaeth, April 19, 1967 (Menil Foundation).

110. A print of the architect's drawing is in the Menil Foundation. The procedure by which the drawing and changes were made was related to J. de Menil by Eugene Aubry on May 1, 1972, and recorded in a memorandum (Menil Foundation).

111. See Alley, 1981, pp. 657–663.

112. Aubry, 1979 (interview).

The Making of the Chapel:
The Building

The master plan for the University of St. Thomas published in 1959 *(fig. 24)* projected a series of buildings surrounding a central mall. The plan's author, Philip Johnson, wrote:

> St. Thomas is a formal design that consciously follows Jefferson's University of Virginia plan as a model, but has a less open character. There will be an inner cloister walk connecting all the buildings and the complex will be built within and against a cityscape. With all the buildings facing inward to the sheltered walk, the campus proper will form more of a "garden street" than a typical American campus. The strong sense of community which would result is the same sense of cohesion a cloister gives a monastery.[113] *(fig. 45)*

Since the college was administered by the Basilian Fathers, Johnson's analogy of the campus with a monastic community was not inappropriate. From the beginning, a chapel had been foreseen as an important building in the campus complex. The first business of the new university was education, however, and the earliest buildings constructed contained classrooms and an auditorium. While the university developed and funds were being sought to construct the projected buildings, several neighborhood houses around the campus site were renovated to accommodate other services. One of these older structures was transformed by Glen Heim into a small chapel overlooking an enclosed garden, and it has served the university ever since.

The Basilian fathers were eager for a large chapel to be built on the campus mall, and Philip Johnson was also thinking along those

lines. Johnson's idea was to have a chapel that would "dominate the ensemble [on the mall] by virtue of its height and placement."[114] It was to be a large square structure, placed centrally so that it terminated one end of the mall.

After Rothko was given the commission for the chapel paintings in 1964, he was brought into the discussions regarding the architectural design of the building. As we have seen, with his participation the plan of the interior evolved rapidly from a square into an octagon by October 1964. Likewise, the disposition and dimensions of the walls were decided upon in the fall of 1964. Although the stepped, recessed floor originally projected was eliminated, the floor plan and the elevations of the walls never changed from that early design.

In every other respect, however—the design of the building's exterior, its location, and the community it would serve—the chapel underwent a number of changes between 1964 and its dedication in 1971.

45. Philip Johnson, mall, University of St. Thomas, 1962

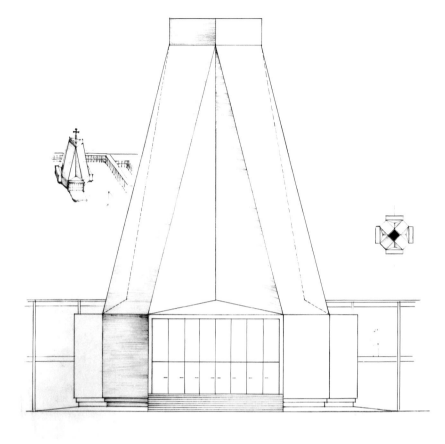

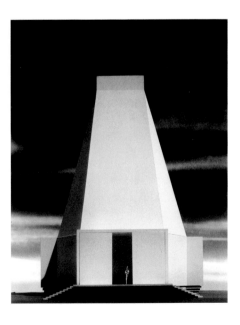

46. Philip Johnson, octagonal plan revised elevation, 1965

47. Philip Johnson, scale model of octagonal plan, 1965

Dated architectural drawings given by Philip Johnson to the Menil Foundation document the evolution of the design. Johnson first envisioned a square block building with an inverted stepped base, set on a platform, and surmounted by a tall pyramid *(fig. 27)*. The building was to be made of concrete, stuccoed and painted white. The capping pyramid would be slightly truncated, its vertex cut off to create an oculus allowing light to enter the building and illuminate the paintings. Le Corbusier's drawings for the Church of St. Pierre de Firminy, dating from late 1962, seem strongly to have influenced this first design—in its square ground plan, in its tall, tapered superstructure opened with an oculus, and in its use of concrete. [115]

When Johnson and Rothko decided upon an octagonal disposition of the interior walls, Johnson altered the design of the exterior somewhat, while retaining the general concept of a single-story building surmounted by a pyramid. He encased the octagon and its apse in a modified Greek-cross plan: one arm of the cross was the apse, while the other three arms provided space for the vestibule, sacristy, and confessionals (fig. 26). In elevation, this change of ground plan was reflected in a shift from the simplicity of the first project to a more complex geometry (figs. 46, 47). Johnson then explored the rich sculptural potential of the building in a series of designs that show the different forms a polyhedronal pyramid could take. These studies recall the faceted tower of the nuclear reactor Johnson had built in 1960 in Rehovot, Israel.

Johnson incorporated the new chapel design into a revised master plan for the St. Thomas campus (fig. 48). Dated March 2, 1965, this site plan shows the chapel at the center of a cluster of projected buildings. The new scheme was due partly to practical demands, since the university had not yet obtained permission to close off the city street that ran through the mall separating the proposed chapel site from the rest of the campus. The group of buildings that Johnson envisioned around the chapel could exist independently if necessary; or if the closing of the street was granted, it could be united with the rest, forming a lateral, transept-like element terminating the "nave" of the mall.

Johnson's monumental chapel was intended to dominate the campus, differing from the other buildings in every way. While they were made uniformly of Miesian brick, black steel, and glass, the chapel would be built of concrete, plastered and painted white. While the other buildings were simple, modular, and rectilinear in form, the chapel would be complex and angular. Moreover, the chapel would tower over the two-story buildings and colonnade that surrounded it. With its faceted pyramidal superstructure, the chapel would have been like an enormous white cut stone set in a buff-and-black planar mounting (fig. 49).

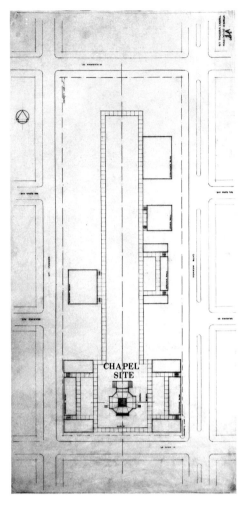

48. Philip Johnson, revised master plan, University of St. Thomas, 1965

49. Philip Johnson, revised mall longitudinal section, University of St. Thomas, 1965

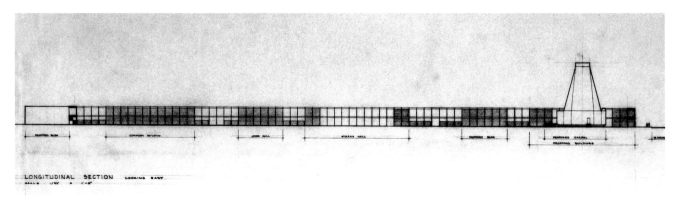

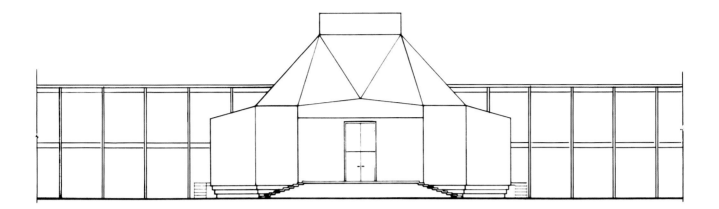

Philip Johnson recalls that when Rothko was shown the architectural designs in progress in fall 1964, the painter was both pleased and displeased. He liked the interior octagonal plan, and the interior walls—their height, and the doors cut into them. The two points on which he challenged Johnson's design, however, were the height of the building, and the manner in which it was to receive light.[116]

As planned by Johnson, the superstructure's soaring height had two rationales. One was practical: although the skylight was relatively small, Johnson thought the light entering through the oculus, reflected on the white inner surface of the pyramidal roof, would provide adequate illumination for the paintings on the walls of the octagon below. The other reason was aesthetic: the height gave the building the grandeur, the monumental presence in the campus ensemble that Johnson had wanted the chapel to have from the beginning—even before Rothko's paintings had come into consideration.

When confronted with Johnson's designs, it became clear that Rothko had a totally different idea about the chapel design. He wanted the building's ceiling to be no higher than that in his Manhattan studio.[117] He also objected to Johnson's tall capping pyramid in terms of its efficacy as a light source. Katharine Kuh believes there was something else at work in his criticisms: Rothko "stubbornly opposed impressive architectural settings for his canvases"; he did so, she felt, "so that the work of art itself might never be overpowered."[118]

Dominique and John de Menil were asked to take sides in the disagreement. They agreed with Rothko, and furthermore had their

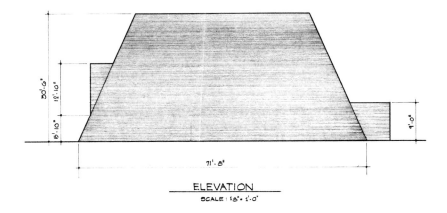

ELEVATION
SCALE : ⅛" = 1'-0"

51. Philip Johnson, truncated pyramid elevation, 1967

52. Philip Johnson, truncated pyramid section, 1967

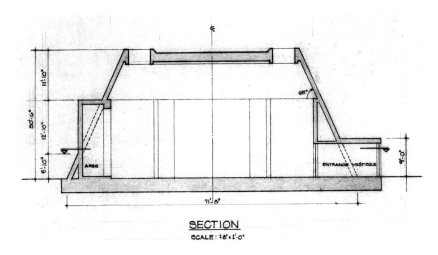

SECTION
SCALE : ⅛" = 1'-0"

own grounds for disapproving the exterior design, feeling strongly that so grand a building as Johnson proposed was not in keeping with the new anti-triumphal stance that the Catholic church had repeatedly affirmed at the Second Vatican Council.[119]

The central oculus with which Johnson proposed to light the chapel has many distinguished historical precedents. Most important among these, of course, is the Pantheon, whose oculus has astonished and entranced visitors to Rome for nearly two thousand years. Rothko did not actually object to a central, overhead light in the chapel, since that was the system that he had in his studio. He was plagued, however, with his characteristic anxiety that the light would be too strong.[120] As we have seen, the question of light was one over which Rothko had contended repeatedly in the

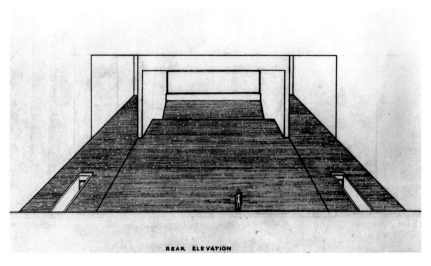

REAR ELEVATION

53. Philip Johnson, berm elevation, 1967

past. He had struggled for, and often obtained, control of lighting conditions when his paintings went on exhibition. He had gone to the effort of personally supervising the hanging and lighting of his works in the homes of private collectors. So when it came to lighting the chapel to house his murals, it might have been expected that he would not yield.

Johnson's designs for the chapel in the following months, and on until 1967, responded to Rothko's criticisms. Johnson first modified the superstructure, then eliminated it; and he introduced different lighting systems. In one project—still for a concrete building—the pyramidal roof is retained, but dramatically shortened *(fig. 50)*. In other designs the use of concrete is abandoned, in favor of a brick-faced exterior to harmonize with the rest of the buildings on the St. Thomas mall. One such design shows the chapel as a truncated pyramid on a square base, with a band of skylights around the roof perimeter *(figs. 51, 52)*; in another project—related to the underground picture gallery Johnson had just built for himself in New Canaan—the chapel is a brick berm, set in a gravel courtyard amid a grove of trees; its flat roof contains a curvilinear cluster of skylights in the center, and rectangular ones at the sides *(figs. 53–55)*. One brick-faced facade design is substantially similar to the final scale and configuration of the chapel *(fig. 56)*.

None of these alternatives calmed Rothko's worries. It became clear that artist and architect had reached an impasse, which Johnson resolved by withdrawing from the project in favor of Howard Barnstone *(fig. 58)*, who was acting as supervising architect on this and other Johnson buildings in Texas. Working in close contact

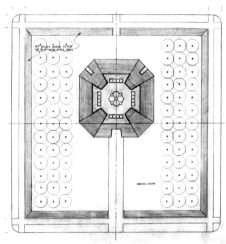

54. Philip Johnson, berm site plan, 1967

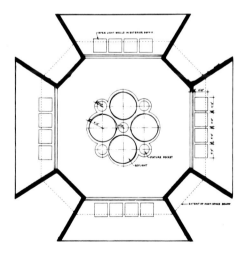

55. Philip Johnson, reflected ceiling plan at clerestory level, 1967

EAST ELEVATION

56. Philip Johnson, brick-faced facade
elevation, 1967

with Rothko, whose opinions on the architecture of the building
they took into careful consideration, Barnstone and his partner Eugene Aubry *(fig. 57)* carried the design to completion. The current
building, a simple octagonal brick structure with a flat roof, reflects
the final design plan that Barnstone and Aubry executed according
to Rothko's ideas *(figs. 59, 60)*.

The foremost concern for Rothko was, as always, how his
paintings were to be lighted. Rothko wanted Barnstone and Aubry
to use an arrangement like the one he had in his own studio, where
the central lantern skylight could be screened on a bright day and
the light diffused through a veil of parachute silk.[121] Rothko's opinion on this matter was based only on his experience in the Manhattan carriage house where he worked; among other things, it did not
take into account the searing and changeable light of the Gulf Coast
city which he had never visited.[122] The contract for the commission
called for Rothko to oversee the installation and the lighting of the
paintings in Houston. Had he lived to do so, adjustments might
have been undertaken with his consultation. As it is, ever since the
opening of the chapel, the lighting has been a problem. It has been
studied, and altered, but never successfully resolved. In 1974 the
original overhead skylight which encompasses the ceiling *(fig. 61)*
was covered with a diffusing scrim *(fig. 62)*. A baffle was added in
1976 to deflect natural light and reduce its level *(fig. 63)*.

Rothko also took an active interest in the finishing details
of the building. He had always abhorred the antiseptic quality of
white walls. For the chapel, he experimented with many different
shades of gray.[123] Finally, he told the architects he wanted his paintings hung on a natural-color, textured surface.[124] It was not to

57. Eugene Aubry, 1965

be painted: Rothko said he wanted only materials in their natural state to be used. As late as February 1970 Rothko was still thinking about this, and in a meeting with Eugene Aubry he suggested using concrete walls; but since construction was already underway, it was too late to implement this idea, so they proceeded with the solution they had agreed upon earlier. The interior walls were made of concrete blocks, with uncolored plaster sprayed on the surface. At the same meeting in February 1970, two weeks before his death, Rothko also approved the final drawings for the building, along with samples of other finishing materials: the brick for the exterior

58. Howard Barnstone, 1965

59. Barnstone and Aubry, plan (as built), 1970

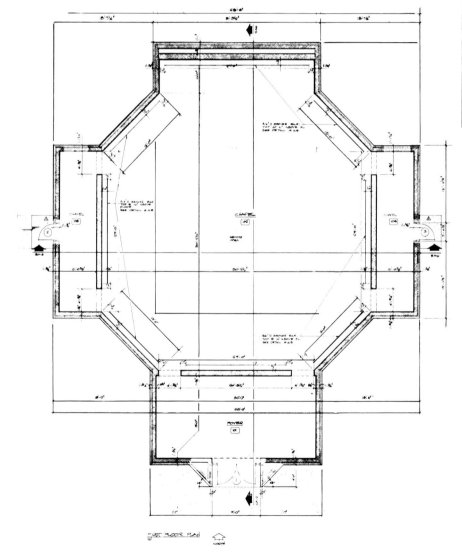

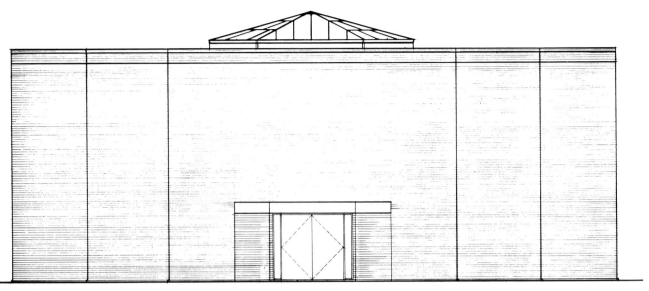

SOUTH ELEVATION
1/4"

facing, and the asphalt blocks that would make up the floor. Aubry also recalls their discussing plans for the dedication of the building; Rothko was "enthusiastic, delightful," and looking forward to traveling to Texas.[125]

After Rothko's death on February 25, 1970, the chapel was completed with the plans and materials that he had endorsed. Howard Barnstone had withdrawn from the project due to illness, leaving Eugene Aubry in charge. Aubry asked Philip Johnson to help as a consultant, and he agreed. Johnson designed the main entrance to the chapel, including the windows that bring daylight into the vestibule; he oriented the chapel on the site; and he designed the reflecting pool for Barnett Newman's sculpture, *Broken Obelisk.*

60. Barnstone and Aubry, elevation (as built), 1970

61. Rothko Chapel (interior), original
skylight grid, 1971

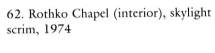

62. Rothko Chapel (interior), skylight scrim, 1974

63. Rothko Chapel (interior), skylight with deflection baffle, 1976

Notes

113. *Architectural Record,* September 1959, p. 180.

114. "Université de St. Thomas," 1963, p. 27 (author's translation).

115. I am very grateful to Mina Marefat for bringing this striking comparison to my attention. Le Corbusier's drawings for Firminy were published in 1964 by the Association Le Corbusier pour la construction de l'Eglise St. Pierre de Firminy with the authorization of the Student Publication of the School of Design, North Carolina State University. See also Eardley, 1981.

116. Johnson, 1979 (interview).

117. Johnson, 1979 (interview).

118. Kuh, 1981 (interview), from the manuscript of her memoirs about Rothko.

119. The commentary to article 24, chapter 3 of the decrees of the Vatican council, issued November 21, 1964, reiterated this stand: "An ecumenical attitude excludes all triumphalism and postulates a humble confession of human powerlessness." (*Das zweite Vatikanische Konzil* 1966–1968, 2: 123 [author's translation]).

The criticism concerning triumphalism was also made by a cleric active in issues of contemporary church design, Dom Frederic Debuyst, a Benedictine monk from Bruges, Belgium and director of *Art d'Eglise,* when he saw Johnson's drawings and the model on a visit to Houston, September 5, 1965 (as noted by D. de Menil, September 5, 1965).

120. Rothko voiced that fear to Herbert Ferber (Ferber, 1981 [interview]).

121. Barnstone, 1978 (personal communication).

122. Dore Ashton (1971, p. 74) wrote, "He said he wanted it to be like his studio, but his studio was so much a part of his mind's eye that I wonder if he really knew what it would look like." Robert Motherwell saw the chapel on the kind of day not uncommon in Houston, when the light changes constantly. He told us he had asked himself then which of the twenty-odd different lighting conditions he had seen in one hour Rothko would have preferred (Motherwell, 1980 [interview]).

123. Edwards, 1977 (interview).

124. Aubry, 1979 (interview).

125. Aubry, 1979 (interview).

The Making of the Chapel:
Broken Obelisk

B *roken Obelisk* stands in a reflecting pool to the south of the Rothko Chapel, on axis with the main entrance to the building. The significance and order of ambition of this monumental sculpture complements the chapel so well that it would seem to have been intended specifically for the site, but *Broken Obelisk* was conceived and executed by Barnett Newman *(fig. 64)* quite independently. John and Dominique de Menil felt it to be a work of tragic grandeur; they brought it to Houston and dedicated it to the slain civil rights leader, Martin Luther King, Jr.

Barnett Newman, who was best known as a painter, recalled having had the idea for *Broken Obelisk* in 1963.[126] At that time, however, he was unable to find anyone with the technical expertise necessary to undertake mounting an inverted obelisk apex-to-apex atop a pyramid. Early in 1967, the sculptor Robert Murray took Newman to the factory of Don Lippincott to see a newly completed piece of Murray's.[127] Lippincott was attracting many artists to work at his new enterprise, because he offered them more control in the execution of their sculptures than did other fabricators, and would finance the production of sculptures as speculative ventures.[128] Murray recalls that Newman and Lippincott got along well from the first. They discussed the problems posed by *Broken Obelisk*, and the reluctance of fabricators to undertake its manufacture in steel.[129]

On subsequent visits, Newman and Lippincott decided to collaborate on *Broken Obelisk*, making drawings *(fig. 65)*, several small

64. Barnett Newman seated in front of
The Stations of the Cross: First Station in
his West End Ave. apartment, New York,
1966

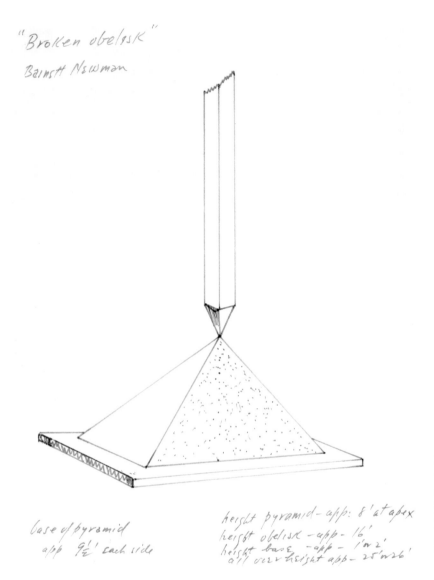

"Broken obelisk"
Barnett Newman

base of pyramid
app 9½' each side

height pyramid - app: 8' at apex
height obelisk - app - 16'
height base - app - 1'or 2'
o'll over height app - 25'or 26'

65. Barnett Newman
Broken Obelisk, 1967
Felt pen on paper
12½ × 9¼ in.
The Menil Collection, Houston

66. Installation of *Broken Obelisk* in front of Rothko Chapel, 1970

cardboard models and finally full-scale mock-ups in cardboard and plywood.[130] The pyramid is composed of four triangles, each having an altitude and a base that measure nine-and-one-half feet. It was fabricated first: Newman himself drew the lines on the steel and supervised its cutting.[131] Then a full-scale mock-up of the obelisk element was made.[132] Once its dimensions were determined, Lippincott and his assistants cut four pieces of Cor-Ten steel plate, all having the width of one side of the obelisk but more than its expected length. Newman drew the jagged lines he desired for the upper broken edge of the obelisk directly onto the steel. These were cut by

Lippincott's men, and the four sides of the obelisk welded together. Finally, Lippincott and his assistants designed the irregularly-shaped cover piece that caps the work. The obelisk is sixteen feet ten inches tall; the total height of the sculpture is twenty-six feet six inches. The point where the obelisk and pyramid meet is a square 2¼ inches per side. A steel rod encased in an internal sleeve joins and aligns the obelisk and pyramid.

In the spring of 1967 two examples of the sculpture were made: the one presently at the Rothko Chapel *(fig. 66)*, and the other now in the collection of University of Washington, Seattle.[133] In response to one of this pair being called a "the second copy of an edition of two," Newman wrote: "I have always made each of my sculptures in an edition of two. . . . both sculptures in the edition are originals. They both were made at the same time and the same place. . . . They are identical twins."[134] In frequent heated debates with Robert Murray and David Smith concerning the pros and cons of editions of sculpture, Newman had liked Murray's proposal that artists make editions of two in order to retain one for themselves. In that way, without engaging in the excessive multiplication of sculptures for which they criticized certain contemporaries, they could guard against the destruction of a unique piece, which particularly concerned David Smith.[135]

It is not clear when Newman decided to have the third example of *Broken Obelisk* made, but it was fabricated sometime before November 1969.[136] It arrived at The Museum of Modern Art in September 1971, where it was installed in the sculpture garden and was included in the museum's Newman retrospective from October 21, 1971 to January 10, 1972.[137]

In *Broken Obelisk,* Newman began with regular geometric shapes: four triangles welded together create the pyramidal base, with four smaller triangles and four rectangles comprising the inverted obelisk. The essential formal regularity of these parts of the sculpture would seem to contradict Newman's frequently-expressed opposition to an art of pure geometry, such as neo-plasticism. As Newman stated:

> . . . Even Mondrian, in his attempt to destroy the Renaissance picture by his insistence on pure subject matter, succeeded only in raising the white plane and right angle into a realm of sublimity, where the sublime paradoxically becomes an absolute of perfect sensations. The geometry (perfection) swallowed up his metaphysics (his exaltation).[138]

67. *Obelisk of Thothmes III,* from the Temple of Heliopolis, Egypt, XVIII Dynasty; now in Central Park, New York

68. Pyramids at Giza, Egypt, IV Dynasty

However, in *Broken Obelisk,* Newman's appreciation of an apparently absolute geometry was crucially informed by its symbolism.

Thomas Hess wrote of Newman's abiding interest in the pyramid, which in ancient Egypt represented the dead king's place of ascent to the sun.[139] Hess notes that the obelisk is also a symbol of life and renewal, representing the sun's rays *(fig. 67)*. *Broken Obelisk* refers quite specifically to the pyramids of Egypt: as Hess noted, the apex angle of the pyramid component closely approximates those of the Great Pyramid at Giza *(fig. 68)* and the Pyramid of Chephren.[140] Robert Murray recalls that Newman was interested in the energy created by the collision of these two Egyptian forms.[141]

Newman's response to the question of scale was as complex as it was to geometry. For him scale was simply not a matter of size; he considered his painting *The Wild* (95¾ × 1⅝ in.) to be as monumental in feeling as *Vir Heroicus Sublimis* (7 ft. 11¼ in. × 17 ft. 9 in.).[142] In its early design stages, when *Broken Obelisk* was still awaiting the proper technology for its fabrication, Newman envisioned the effect of its eventual scale. However, it was not until he had made the full-size mock-up of the pyramidal unit and juncture point that he was convinced of the suitability of their proportions: ". . . since I work directly, I felt I had to see the possibilities in terms of scale, visually. . . ."[143] Although Newman had confronted this issue much earlier in his paintings, *Broken Obelisk* was the first instance where he was faced with the problem of tangible volume on a large scale, and it is noteworthy that he created a simulacrum of the finished product in order to assure a sense of "felt" scale.[144]

Broken Obelisk was born at a moment of changing perceptions about the scale, function and placement of contemporary sculpture. For aesthetic reasons as well as for freedom from the gallery environment and its economic system, a number of younger American sculptors had grown increasingly interested in site-specific commissions for outdoor sculpture.[145] In 1967, however, large-scale abstract sculptures had yet to become commonplace in our cities. One of the exhibitions where *Broken Obelisk* was presented in October 1967, "Sculpture in Environment," was a pioneering venture, placing twenty-nine contemporary sculptures in public spaces around New York City; *Broken Obelisk* was installed on the Seagram Building plaza *(fig. 69)*. That exhibition's organizers anticipated "howls of shock and scattered grumblings of discontent" at the works being set "loose in the city . . . under the light of day where they intrude upon our daily walks and errands".[146] In his introductory essay to the exhibition catalogue, Irving Sandler challenged both

69. *Broken Obelisk,* installed in Seagram Building plaza, New York, 1967

70. *Broken Obelisk,* in reflecting pool, Rothko Chapel, 1971

the artists and the city planners whom he saw as potential patrons to collaborate to "integrate art and the urban environment" in "a new birth of public art."[147]

Broken Obelisk's way to Houston was marked by some of the political and social controversy that characterized the late 1960s.[148] On May 2, 1969, John and Dominique de Menil proposed to the Houston Municipal Art Commission that they provide the funds, which had not been found, to match a grant from the National Foundation on the Arts and Humanities for the purchase of a work of contemporary sculpture. They specified that the work be *Broken Obelisk,* that it be placed near City Hall, and that it be dedicated to Dr. Martin Luther King, Jr. Although the Municipal Art Commission endorsed the proposal, they chose to neither endorse nor reject its dedication, and in the following weeks the mayor and city councilmen resolved not to accept the sculpture with the dedication to King. Late in August, the de Menils decided to withdraw their offer and to purchase the sculpture outright.

In November 1969, Barnett Newman and his wife Annalee came to Houston to help the de Menils search for the proper place for *Broken Obelisk*. After they viewed several locations, it suddenly became clear to them that the sculpture should share the site of the Rothko Chapel, for which construction was presently to begin. Barnett Newman then took part in the design of the reflecting pool which he wanted to accompany the sculpture, and in the pool's placement on the grounds *(figs. 70, 71)*. After the sculpture arrived on October 27, 1970, according to Newman's wishes it was sandblasted so that a new patina would form in response to the atmosphere of its final home. Thus *Broken Obelisk* came to be a vital element of the Rothko Chapel, bringing together complementary masterpieces of post-war American art.

71. *Broken Obelisk* at night, Rothko Chapel

Notes

126. Newman, 1968. In addition to published information (Hess, 1971, pp. 120–123, and Alloway, 1971, p. 23), this account is based on the recollections of Robert Murray and Don Lippincott (telephone conversations with Peter Lukehart in October and November 1986, and January 1987), to whom we are most grateful. Unfortunately, Mr. Lippincott's records for the period up to 1970 seem to have been lost.

127. Murray, November 1986 (personal communication).

128. For more on the early days of Lippincott, Inc., see B. Rose, 1968, pp. 87–91.

129. Lippincott, November 1986 (personal communication).

130. According to Lippincott (October 1986 [personal communication]), plans for the sculpture were sketched by Newman, then redrawn by Lippincott's staff at his center; in the early stages of the design, drawings were sent back and forth between Lippincott and Newman. One drawing by Newman (*fig. 65*), now in The Menil Collection, was exhibited in "Drawings for Outdoor Sculpture 1946–1977," at John Weber Gallery, New York, and illustrated (cropped at the bottom) in the unpaginated checklist (Singer, 1977; see also Richardson, 1979, p. 210). Alloway (1971, pp. 22–23) describes that drawing and discusses the working process with the models.

131. Lippincott, November 1986 (personal communication).

132. Lippincott, January 1987 (personal communication). According to Lippincott, no full-scale mock-up of the obelisk unit was made, contrary to Alloway, 1971, p. 23.

133. Contrary to information published in 1971 (Rosenberg, 1971, n.p.), the piece in Seattle is not numbered on the metal surface of the sculpture. Neither are those in Houston and New York, although a drawing from Lippincott in the files of The Museum of Modern Art carries the number '3/3'. According to Lippincott (January 1987 [personal communication]), he and Newman discussed, but never undertook, the possibility of fabricating an even larger example of *Broken Obelisk*.

134. Newman (letter to the Editor, *Artforum*), 1968, p. 4.

135. Murray, November 1986 (personal communication).

136. Annalee Newman states that an edition of three was always intended for *Broken Obelisk* (October 1986 [personal communication]). Hess wrote that after *Here I* and *Here II*, which were in editions of two, Newman's remaining sculptures were made in editions of three (Hess, 1971, pp. 119–120). I am grateful to Judith Cousins of the Department of Painting and Sculpture, The Museum of Modern Art (November 1986 [personal communication]), who confirmed that Don Lippincott retained an invoice dated November 13, 1969 for the third example. Robert Murray (December 1986 [personal communication]) suggested that, because there was no immediate deadline for its completion, the third example could have been fabricated over the course of 1968–1969.

137. From 1967 to 1970, the different examples of *Broken Obelisk* appeared in various exhibitions around the country. The first two were shown almost simultaneously in the fall of 1967: one in New York on the Seagram Building

plaza as part of "Sculpture in Environment," New York City Parks, Recreation and Cultural Affairs Administration for the Cultural Showcase Festival (October 1–31, 1967); the other outside the Corcoran Gallery in Washington, D.C. in the exhibition "Scale as Content" (October 7, 1967–January 7, 1968). Even though the latter exhibition officially concluded early in 1968, Newman left *Broken Obelisk* at the Corcoran on extended loan, not removing it until July 11, 1969. Other exhibitions where an example of the sculpture was shown include: "Sculpture Downtown," sponsored by the Michigan State Council for the Arts, in Detroit (June 1969); and "New York Painting and Sculpture: 1940–1970," Metropolitan Museum of Art, New York (October 18, 1969–February 1, 1970), where it was exhibited along the south wall of the museum at 80th Street and 5th Ave. (Geldzahler, 1987 [personal communication]). See Rosenberg, 1971, n.p. Between showings, the works were stored at Lippincott's factory, where they were sandblasted, leaving no visual evidence to indicate which examples were included in specific exhibitions.

138. (Newman, Dec. 1948, p. 52; see also Lippard, 1968, pp. 42–43 and Hopps, São Paolo, 1965, n.p., catalogue essay on Newman). This apparent contradiction of Newman's historic condemnation of geometry needs clarification. Beginning in the 1940s Newman expressed a contempt for received notions of geometry in art, both in his paintings such as *Euclidean Abyss* (1947, Collection Mr. and Mrs. E. Cohen) and in writings such as "The First Man was an Artist" (Oct. 1947, pp. 57–60) and "The Sublime is Now" (Dec. 1948, pp. 51–53). Newman's animosity towards the strict adherence to mathematical formulas persisted in his statements through the 1960s, although over the course of his career the focus of his criticism shifted from Mondrian and the followers of neo-plasticism to artists such as Albers and Vasarely. In 1968, After studying Cimabue's *Madonna and Child* Newman remarked that: " . . . It is not only the heart that's at work here, but the mind. Not Vasarely's and Albers' kind of intelligence. The insulting thing about these guys is that they feel they have a mortgage on the mind. And they reduce it to a table of logarithms." (Schneider, 1969, p. 38). Newman's criticism of his contemporaries must be considered before one can begin to comprehend the intended complexity of his own artistic statement.

The irregular incisions at the base of the pyramid and the jagged upper edge of *Broken Obelisk* reveal the artist's hand and further modify the work's otherwise regular geometry (Alloway, 1971, pp. 23–24). This is an issue not only in *Broken Obelisk,* but also in much of Newman's work. For example, in an effort to deflect the strict symmetry of his triangular canvases *Jericho* and *Chartres* (both 1968–1969), Newman deliberately set the "stripe" divisions of the paintings off-center (Newman, 1969, p. 29). Further, Newman chose a material for his sculpture which he knew would weather irregularly, so that each surface might assume an individualized character over the course of time (Don Lippincott, October and November 1986 [personal communication]). Through such interpositions, Newman aspired to create what he termed a "post-geometric" style (Lippard, 1968, p. 42).

139. "The Pyramid texts often describe the king as mounting to heaven on the rays of the sun. . . . The temptation to regard the true pyramid as a material representation of the sun's rays and consequently as a means whereby the dead king could ascend to heaven seems irresistible." (Edwards, 1961, p. 291). Newman owned two copies of the 1947 edition of Edwards' book (Hess, 1971, p. 121).

140. Hess, 1971, p. 121. The apex angle on *Broken Obelisk* is 53°. That of the Great Pyramid is 51° 52', and that of the Pyramid of Chephren is 52° 20'.

141. Robert Murray (November 1986 [personal communication]) reiterated Hess's observation (1971, pp. 122–123) that Newman was quite fond of the Obelisk of Thothmes III, generally referred to as "Cleopatra's Needle"; Murray and Newman often visited Central Park in order to see it. According to Murray, Newman was also enthralled with Egyptian sculpture, whose solidity, essential forms, and architectural dependence he found pleasing; yet at the same time, he criticized the Egyptians for the lack of humanity expressed in their works.

It should be noted that there is a visual precedent for the arrangement of a pyramid and a superimposed obelisk in a painting by Rudolf Bauer, *Blue Triangle,* 1934 (New York, Solomon R. Guggenheim Museum). *Blue Triangle* was exhibited at the Guggenheim Museum in "Art of Tomorrow" (1939), and was illustrated in the catalogue (no. 153, p. 107). See also Rudenstine, 1976, 1:32 and Neuberger, 1985, p. 77, fig. 50. I am grateful to Annette Schlagenhauff for bringing to my attention this possible source for *Broken Obelisk*.

142. Radio interview, WNET-FM, 1966; see also Newman's interview with Andrew Hudson, 1966, G-11. *The Wild,* ill. Hess, 1972, p. 45 n. 26; *Vir Heroicus Sublimus,* ill. MoMA, 1984, p. 213, n. 314. Newman's reactions to the works of the great masters shed light on his own definition of scale. Touring the Louvre with Pierre Schneider, Newman commented upon two paintings which treated scale with varying degrees of success. The first was Veronese's *Marriage at Cana,* which failed to impress Newman with its scale, despite its colossal proportions: "Here is a symmetrical painting that doesn't work. It is so symmetrical that the symmetry overshadows everything. . . . Also, it's fussy. It is really a small painting, that's the trouble." (Schneider, 1969, p. 38). At the same museum, however, Newman praised, in a tone which was at once one of admiration and self-recognition, Géricault's *Raft of the Medusa* in which ". . . The scale is marvelous. You feel the immensity of the event rather than the size of the painting. The space does engulf one. . . ." (Schneider, 1969, p. 70); see also the discussion of scale in Lippard, 1968, pp. 42–43.

143. Newman, March 1968, p. 4; Lippincott, Jan. 1987 (personal communication).

144. Radio interview, Slate, 1966; Hudson, 1966.

145. Sandler, 1967, n.p. See Rose, 1968, p. 80 on the reasons for "the dearth of monumental sculpture in the modern period" until that time.

146. Heckscher, 1967, n.p.

147. Sandler, 1967, n.p.

148. This account is based on documents in the Menil Foundation.

Rothko Chapel (exterior), 1971

A Sacred Place

72–74. *(clockwise from top)* Crane hoisting wrapped paintings during chapel installation, 1970

A Sacred Place:
The Installation and Dedication

Anyone who happened to be in the neighborhood of the Rothko Chapel when the paintings were delivered in 1970 will never forget the sight. The panels had been taken from Rothko's studio in 1967 on their stretchers. On stretchers they had remained in storage, and on stretchers they were shipped. Because of the great size of the plum-colored monochromes, each measuring over fourteen by eleven feet, no standard moving van could transport the paintings. A unique over-sized truck, owned by two men who specialized in moving large art works, was engaged. The extraordinary height of the truck, in turn, required special precautions en route from New York to Houston— on the highway, low underpasses had to be anticipated and avoided; in the city of Houston, the path was charted with attention to overhead telephone and electric lines.

The truck's arrival was itself cause enough for excitement, but could not compare with the spectacle to follow, for the only way for the large canvases to be taken into the building was through the roof. This had long been foreseen, and the skylight had been designed in wedge-like sections, one of which was removed to admit the paintings. E.G. Lowry Construction Company, the firm that had built the chapel, provided a crane with a large sling to carry the paintings. The sling was to be anchored with guy wires held by several men standing at different points on the roof of the building, inside it, and on the ground outside. Everything was ready for the installation on the day the truck arrived, but the weather forced postponement—Houston was beset with gusty winds that

75. Lowering of painting through chapel skylight, 1970

76. *Broken Obelisk* dedication—address of Dominique de Menil, *(seated left to right)* Dr. Thompson Shannon, Rev. W. Lawson, Sheikh Subhy el Saleh and the Texas Southern University Choir, February 28, 1971

would have carried the canvases in their sling through the air like giant sails. The next day, in the still of the early morning after the winds had subsided, one by one the paintings were set in the sling, lifted by the crane *(figs. 72–74)*, and guided gently down through the open section of the skylight into the building *(fig. 75)*. The largest of them cleared the opening by only a few inches. A team of experts from the Rice University Museum—L. D. Dreyer, Jesse Lopez, and Jim Love—hung the paintings under Mrs. de Menil's direction, following the instructions that Rothko had given when they had left his studio in 1967.

On February 27 and 28, 1971, in two solemn yet festive ceremonies attended by dignitaries of different faiths and countries, the Rothko Chapel and *Broken Obelisk* were dedicated *(fig. 76)*. From the beginning, the Rothko Chapel addressed itself to an international community. The celebrants brought together by Dr. Thompson Shannon for the consecration of the chapel included Cardinal Willebrands of the Vatican, and the Rev. Eugene S. Smith of the World Council of Churches, as well as representatives of Jewish, Muslim, Greek Orthodox, and Protestant denominations *(fig. 77)*.

A low, simple, concrete-block structure, its outside faced with brick, its gray-plastered interior walls bearing only the paintings that Rothko had made for that space—in a way, the chapel was the realization of the dream that Rothko had spoken of to Herbert Ferber and Mrs. Gifford Phillips so many years before: the simple, environmental, one-man museum.

77. Chapel dedication, *(left to right)* Rev. Eugene S. Smith, Prof. Albert C. Outler and Cardinal Willebrands, February 27, 1971

A Sacred Place:
Postscript – The Institution

I n the years between 1967 and 1971, discussions had taken place between the de Menils and the University of St. Thomas administration that had changed the destiny of the chapel as an institution.

Since the death of Jermayne MacAgy in 1964, the St. Thomas Art Department had been headed by Dominique de Menil, and it had continued to grow. By 1968 it was clear that the development of the Art Department, with the de Menils' patronage, had far outpaced that of the other programs at St. Thomas. The Basilian fathers felt that the arts on campus were eclipsing the core studies of philosophy and theology to which the university was primarily dedicated. Nevertheless, the de Menils showed no signs of curtailing their activity. Nearby Rice University, on the other hand, which had for fifty years based its national standing on science and engineering studies, was developing its curriculum in the arts and humanities. The administration at Rice was eager to expand its own art department by acquiring the program from St. Thomas. An agreement between the two universities and the de Menils was reached, and in the fall of 1969 the art history faculty, the exhibition program, art library and slide library, and the media studies center—all of which the de Menils had developed and supported—were transferred from the University of St. Thomas to Rice University, and a limited exchange program of courses in the arts was established between the neighboring schools.

When the move was first discussed, the de Menils assumed that the chapel would still be built on the St. Thomas campus, and they reaffirmed their support for the project to the Basilian fathers.[149] It soon became clear to all concerned, however, that the fathers could not treat it as they would an ordinary university chapel. The building was going to contain a unique group of mural paintings by a master of contemporary art, an ensemble which Rothko himself believed to be his masterpiece.[150] The responsibility for caring for the works of art and making them available to the public would be too great a burden for the University of St. Thomas to assume. Another solution had to be found.

When it was decided not to build the chapel at St. Thomas, the de Menils, who had always conceived of the chapel as part of the university rather than as an autonomous entity, sought to donate it to another institution. John de Menil was on the board of the Institute for Religion and Human Development in Houston, and he had a close working friendship with its President, Dr. Thompson L. Shannon.[151] The Institute for Religion, located in Houston's Texas Medical Center, is an ecumenical institution devoted to the clinical aspects of pastoral training. The de Menils thought that the chapel might serve the Institute as well as the city, and their offer was accepted by the trustees of the Institute by August, 1969. Together Dr. Shannon and Mr. de Menil undertook the search for a site for the projected chapel; although Dr. Shannon had wanted it to be built in the Texas Medical Center, not enough land was available there, so they decided upon a piece of property which the

78. Buddhist monk preparing to perform wedding ceremony in Rothko Chapel, 1973

79. Whirling dervishes from Turkey performing in front of Rothko Chapel, 1978

de Menils owned in the neighborhood just west of the University of St. Thomas. Located near enough to the Medical Center for the Institute, it was also next to St. Thomas so that the school could make use of the chapel as well, thus partially fulfilling the original intention.

The de Menils' decision to build the chapel under the auspices of the Institute for Religion of course made a decisive difference in the future life of the chapel. This tie with the Institute engendered and nurtured the ecumenical destiny of the chapel *(figs. 78, 79)*. The change posed no problem as regarded the murals. On the contrary: Rothko's paintings, whose meaning was intended to be universal, had always been of ecumenical spirit in the deepest sense.

The Rothko Chapel was affiliated with the Institute for Religion and Human Development from 1969 until late in 1972. By then, the trustees and the administration of the Institute had become convinced that for the full development of its potential, the chapel should become autonomous. The programs of the Institute and the chapel were congenial, but different in nature. The Institute's orientation was academic and scientific, and focused on the Medical Center. On the other hand, since the dedication in early 1971 the activities organized at the Rothko Chapel, with the continuing sponsorship of the de Menils, were most often of an ecumenical religious character. Plans were underway for the first

80. Pandit Pran Nath chanting *Morning Ragas*, Rothko Chapel, 1980

81. Jonas Salk speaking at *Human Rights, Human Reality,* Rothko Chapel Colloquium II, December 1973

of the ongoing series of colloquia held at the chapel addressing themselves to global issues, and including participants from many different countries and cultures *(figs. 81, 83)*. In short, the Institute and the Rothko Chapel each had a unique mission, missions that they would best fulfill by becoming distinct entities.

On October 3, 1972 the Board of Trustees of the Institute for Religion and Human Development approved a resolution transferring the title of the chapel to the Rothko Chapel, Incorporated. Article IV of this incorporation charter states that the Rothko Chapel is "to provide a place of worship, a place of meditation and prayer for people to gather and explore spiritual bonds common to all, to discuss human problems of world-wide interest, and also share a spiritual experience, each loyal to his belief, each respectful of the beliefs of others."[152]

The Rothko Chapel thus took a course that no one had foreseen when it was commissioned in 1964. It became the world's first broadly ecumenical center, a holy place open to all religions and belonging to none. It became a setting for international cultural, religious, and philosophical exchange, for colloquia and performances *(figs. 80, 82, 84)*. And it became a place of private prayer for innumerable individuals of all faiths.

Since its dedication in 1971, the Rothko Chapel stands as a place of worship and meditation, a forum for the advancement of human rights in the world, and living proof of mutual religious understanding and the common humanity in which we share.

82. Steve Reich *(second from right)*, performing *Tehellim,* Rothko Chapel, 1984

83. *Ethnicities and Nations,* Rothko Chapel Colloquium V, October 1983

Notes

149. J. de Menil, letter to Reverend Patrick O. Braden, C.S.B., President of the University of St. Thomas, August 7, 1968.

150. Kuh, 1981 (interview).

151. The following account is drawn from conversations between the author and Dr. Shannon. Dr. Shannon left the Institute for Religion in 1973 to become Director of the Consortium for the University of Oregon Medical School, Portland. He maintained his position on the Board of the chapel, and returned to Houston in 1982 as Executive Director of the Rothko Chapel. See also the accounts in the newspapers: Holmes, 1969; Richard, 1969; and Ferretti, 1969.

152. The incorporators were Reuben W. Askanase, John de Menil and Thompson L. Shannon. The initial Board of Directors was: John de Menil, President; Reuben W. Askanase, Nabila Drooby, Roberto Rossellini, Thompson L. Shannon (chartered in the State of Texas, Charter 313813). Anne Mead was the initial Administrator.

84. His Holiness the Dalai Lama, Rothko Chapel, 1979

Selected Bibliography

Alley, Ronald. *Catalogue of The Tate Gallery's Collection of Modern Art.* London: The Tate Gallery and Sotheby Parke-Bernet, 1981.

Alloway, Lawrence. "Art." *The Nation,* March 15, 1971: 349–350.

——. "One Sculpture." *Arts Magazine,* vol. 48, no. 8 (May 1971): 22–24; and correction *Arts Magazine,* vol. 48, no. 10 (Summer 1971): 64.

——. "Residual Sign Systems in Abstract Expressionism." *Artforum,* vol. 12, no. 9 (November 1973): 36–42.

Ashbery, John and Tessa Namuth. "Houston Comes to Paris: The Amazing Menil Collection is Unveiled not at Home but Abroad." *Newsweek,* April 23, 1984: 60–61.

——. "The Eyes of Texas." *Newsweek,* April 23, 1984: 62.

Ashton, Dore. "The Rothko Chapel in Houston." *Studio International,* vol. 181 (June 1971): 273–275.

——. *The New York School. A Cultural Reckoning.* New York: Penguin Books, 1983. (Originally published under the title *The Life and Times of the New York School: American Painting in the Twentieth Century.* London: Adams and Dart, 1972.)

——. *About Rothko.* New York: Oxford University Press, 1983.

Baker, Elizabeth C. "Barnett Newman in a New Light." *Art News,* vol. 67, no. 10 (February 1969): 38–41; 60–64.

Baro, Gene. "American Sculpture: A New Scene." *Studio International,* vol. 175, no. 896 (January 1968): 9–19.

Barr, Alfred H., ed. *The New American Painting as Shown in Eight European Countries, 1958–59.* exhib. cat. (traveling 1958–1959). New York: Museum of Modern Art, 1969.

Beauchamp, Toni R. "James Johnson Sweeney and the Museum of Fine Arts, 1961–1967." M.A. thesis, University of Texas at Austin, 1983.

Bowling, Frank. "Problems of Criticism: V." *Arts,* vol. 46, no. 7 (May 1972): 37–38.

Breerette, Geneviève. "Dans les jardins de Houston." *Le Monde,* April 12, 1984.

Butor, Michel. "The Mosques of New York or the Art of Mark Rothko." In *Inventory. Essays.* New York: Simon and Schuster, 1968: 7–25.

Carmean, E. A., Jr. "The Church Project: Pollock's Passion Themes." *Art in America,* vol. 70, no. 6 (Summer 1982): 100–122.

"City Seeks Services of Famous Sculptor." *Houston Post,* August 21, 1969.

"A City's Good Fortune." *Houston Post,* February 12, 1971 (editorial section).

Clearwater, Bonnie. *Mark Rothko Works on Paper.* exhib. cat. (traveling June 1984–September 1986). New York: Hudson Hills Press with the Rothko Foundation and the American Federation of Artists, 1984.

——. "How Rothko Looked at Rothko." *Art News,* vol. 84, no. 9 (Nov. 1985): 100–103.

Cohn, Marjorie B., ed. *Mark Rothko's Harvard Murals.* Cambridge, MA: Center for Conservation and Technical Studies. Harvard University Art Museums, 1988.

"College Buildings. St. Thomas. First Units in the Fabric of a Closed Campus." *Architectural Record,* vol. 126, no. 3 (September 1959): 180–183.

Congar, Yves Marie Joseph. *Chrétiens désunis, principes d'un "œcuménisme" catholique.* Paris: Editions du Cerf, 1937.

——. *Divided Christendom: Principles of a Catholic "Ecumenism."* London: G. Bles, 1939.

Corcoran Gallery of Art. *Annual Report of the One Hundred and Ninth Year.* [Washington, D.C.: The Corcoran Gallery of Art, 1968].

"Corcoran Gallery Director to Quit." *Washington Post,* June 29, 1969, D1: col. 1.

"Corcoran's Awesome Sculpture." *Evening Star,* October 5, 1967: B1 (illus.).

"Council Turns to Moon in King Sculpture Debate." *Houston Chronicle,* August 21, 1969.

Couturier, Marie-Alain. "A Note by Father Couturier." *Liturgical Arts,* February 1951: 30–31.

——. *La vérité blessée.* Paris: Plon, 1984.

D'Antonio, Emile, director. [Film interviews] *Painters Painting.* New York: Turin Film Corp., 1970.

Davidson, Spenser. "After the Rothko Scandal, an Old Friend Guards the Goods." *Avenue* (New York), March 1982: 110–131.

De Franclieu, Françoise. *Le Corbusier Sketchbooks.* vol. 4 (1957–1964). Cambridge, MA: MIT Press, 1982.

Dillenberger, Jane. *Secular Art with Sacred Themes.* Nashville: Abingdon Press, 1969.

Eardley, Anthony. *Le Corbusier's Firminy Church.* exhib. cat. New York, Institute for Architecture and Urban Studies (April 29–June 3, 1981). New York: Rizzoli, 1981.

Edwards, I. E. S. *The Pyramids of Egypt.* Harmondsworth, Middlesex: Penguin Books, 1949 (rpt. 1961).

Edwards, Roy & Ralph Pomeroy. "Working with Rothko. A Conversation Between Roy Edwards and Ralph Pomeroy." *New American Review,* no. 12 (1971): 109–121.

Ennis, Michael. "Mrs. de Menil's Eye." *Texas Monthly,* July 1984: 116–21, 172–174.

Ferretti, Fred. "Houston Getting a Sculpture after All." *New York Times,* August 16, 1969.

Fischer, John. "Mark Rothko. Portrait of the Artist as an Angry Man." *Harpers Magazine,* July 1970: 16–23.

Forgey, Benjamin. "The Corcoran Show: How to Dig the Big." *Sunday Star,* October 15, 1967: E1: cols. 1–3, E3: cols. 1–4.

Freed, Eleanor. "Dominique de Menil: Rare Vision in the Arts." *Texas Humanist,* September-October 1984: 42–46.

Geldzahler, Henry. *New York Painting and Sculpture: 1940-1970.* exhib. cat. Metropolitan Museum of Art (October 1, 1969–February 1, 1970). New York: E. P. Dutton and the Metropolitan Museum of Art, 1969.

"Geometry Weds Wood." *Washington Post,* September 19, 1967: B1: cols. 1–2.

Gettlein, Frank. "Something for Everyone in New Art Season." *Sunday Star,* September 10, 1967: D1: cols. 1–6; D-3 cols. 4–6.

——. "Harithas is Quitting Corcoran Position." *Washington Star,* June 26, 1969: A2: cols. 4–5.

——. "Gallery Director's Job is not an Easy One." *Washington Star,* July 6, 1969: E1: cols. 1–3; E3: col. 6.

Glueck, Grace. "France Lauds U.S. Family of Art Patrons." *New York Times,* April 19, 1984: C13: cols. 1–6.

——. "The de Menil Family. The Medici of Modern Art." *New York Times Magazine,* May 18, 1986: 28–46, 66, 106, 113.

Goldwater, Robert. "Reflections on the Rothko Exhibition." *Arts,* vol. 35, no. 6 (March 1961): 42–45.

——. "Rothko's Black Paintings." *Art in America,* vol. 59, no. 2 (March-April 1971): 58–63.

Goosen, E. C. *Herbert Ferber.* New York: Abbeville Press, 1981.

Grabar, André. *Martyrium.* 2 vols. London: Variorum Reprints, 1972.

Green, Eleanor. *Scale as Content: Ronald Bladen, Barnett Newman, Tony Smith.* exhib. cat. Washington, D.C., The Corcoran Gallery of Art (October 6, 1967–January 7, 1968). Washington, D.C.: Corcoran Gallery of Art, 1967.

Guillory, Ferrel. "Why Corcoran Director Quit." *Washington Post,* June 30, 1969: B1: cols. 5–6.

Hamilton, John Arnott. *Byzantine Architecture and Decoration.* London: B. T. Batsford, Ltd. [1933].

Heckscher, August. Foreword to *Sculpture in Environment,* exhib. cat. New York, New York Administration of Recreation and Cultural Affairs for the Cultural Showcase Festival (October 1–31, 1967). New York: Stern Brothers for the Department of Parks, Recreation and Cultural Affairs, 1967.

Hess, Thomas B. "New Man in Town." *Art News,* vol. 66, no. 7 (November 1967): 27.

——. *Barnett Newman.* exhib. cat. New York, Knoedler and Company (March 25–April 19, 1969). New York: Walker and Co., 1968.

——. "Mark Rothko 1903–70." *Art News,* vol. 69, no. 2 (April 1970): 29, 66.

——. "Rothko: A Venetian Souvenir." *Art News,* vol. 69, no. 7 (November 1970): 40, 70–74.

——. "Editorial: Can Art Be Used?" *Art News,* vol. 70, no. 2 (April 1971): 33.

——. *Barnett Newman.* exhib. cat. New York, The Museum of Modern Art (October 21, 1971–January 10, 1972). New York: The Museum of Modern Art, 1971.

——. *Barnett Newman.* exhib. cat. London, The Tate Gallery (June 28-August 6, 1972). London: Tate Gallery Publications, 1972.

Heynen, Julian. *Barnett Newmans Texte zur Kunst.* New York: Georg Olms Verlag, Hildesheim, 1979. [1976 diss. for the Technische Hochschule, Aachen.]

Hobbs, Robert Carleton and Levin, Gail. *Abstract Expressionism. The Formative Years.* exhib. cat. (traveling March–December 1978). Ithaca, NY and London, England: Cornell University Press, 1978.

Hoffmann, Ellen. "Artist Barnett Newman Dies." *Washington Post,* July 6, 1970.

"Home for the Obelisk." *Houston Chronicle,* October 28, 1970: 4: 6.

Hudson, Andrew. "Newman Brings Grandeur to Town." *Washington Post,* January 30, 1966: G9: cols. 5–8.

——. "Shows are Rich in Comparison." *Washington Post,* May 21, 1966: H8: cols. 4–7.

——. "Another Promising Art Season is in Store for the Capital." *Washington Post,* August 20, 1967: H7: cols. 1–8.

——. "Scale as Content. Bladen, Newman, Smith at the Corcoran." *Artforum,* vol. 6, no. 4 (December 1967): 46–47.

Jacobus, John M. *Philip Johnson.* New York: G. Braziller, 1962.

Jermayne MacAgy. A Life Illustrated by an Exhibition. exhib. cat. Houston, University of St. Thomas (November 1968–January 1969). Houston: University of St. Thomas, 1968.

Johnston, Marguerite. "The de Menils." *The Houston Post.* January 9–12, 1977.

Johnson, Philip. *Architecture 1949-65.* New York: Holt, Rinehart & Winston, 1966.

Kernan, Michael. "Harithas: Too Exciting." *Washington Post,* July 1, 1969: B3: cols. 1–4.

Knoedler, M. and Co. Invoice of the sale of *Broken Obelisk* to Rothko Chapel in Houston, November 3, 1969. Photocopy in the Menil Foundation (Archive).

Komonchak, Joseph A. "The Return of Yves Congar." *Commonweal,* July 15, 1983: 402–405.

Krautheimer, Richard. *Early Christian and Byzantine Architecture.* Harmondsworth: Penguin, 1965.

Kuh, Katharine. "Farewell to Dogma." *Saturday Review,* August 31, 1968: 32–34.

——. "A Maximum of Poignancy." *Saturday Review,* April 17, 1971: 52, 81.

Legg, Alicia, ed. *Painting and Sculpture in The Museum of Modern Art with Selected Works on Paper.* New York: The Museum of Modern Art, 1977.

Lippard, Lucy. "Escalation in Washington". *Art International,* vol. 12, no. 1 (January 1968): 42–46.

Liss, Joseph. "Willem de Kooning Remembers Mark Rothko." *Art News,* vol. 78, no. 1 (January 1979): 41–44.

Marandel, Jean Patrice. "Une chapelle œcuménique au Texas." *l'Oeil,* no. 197 (May 1971): 16–18.

Mark Rothko 1903-1970, exhib. cat. London, Tate Gallery (June 17–September 1, 1987). London: Tate Gallery Publications, 1987.

Marshall, Neil. *Robert Murray: a Sculpture Exhibition.* exhib. cat. Dayton, Ohio, Dayton Art Institute (May 11–July 8, 1979). Dayton, OH: Dayton Art Institute, 1979.

McShine, Kynaston, ed. *The Natural Paradise. Painting in America 1800-1950.* New York: The Museum of Modern Art, 1976. Essays by Barbara Novak, Robert Rosenblum, John Wilmerding.

Mellow, James R. "New York" (review of "Sculpture in Environment" [October 1–31, 1967]). *Art International,* vol. 11, no. 9 (November 1967): 58–59.

Menil, Dominique de. "Impressions américaines en France," *l'Art Sacré,* nos. 7–8 (March–April 1953): 2–31.

——. "The Rothko Chapel." *Art Journal,* vol. 30, no. 3 (Spring 1971): 249–251.

——. Address at the Rothko Chapel, February 3, 1977. Menil Foundation.

Minnix, Bruce, director. [Film interview] *The Continuity of Vision. Barnett Newman*. New York, Educational Broadcasting Corp., Channel 13 WNET, 1964.

"Monumental." *Washington Post,* September 29, 1967: B8 (ill.).

The Museum of Modern Art. *The Museum of Modern Art Annual Report 1970–1971.* New York: The Museum of Modern Art, 1971.

——. *The Museum of Modern Art Annual Report 1971–1972.* New York: The Museum of Modern Art, 1972.

——. *The Museum of Modern Art, New York. The History of the Collection.* New York: Harry N. Abrams and The Museum of Modern Art, 1984.

The 1958–59 Murals: Second Series. exhib. cat. New York, Pace Gallery (October 28–November 25, 1978). New York: Pace Gallery, 1978.

Nodelman, Sheldon. *Marden, Novros, Rothko: Painting in the Age of Actuality.* Houston, Texas, Institute for the Arts, Rice University (April 18–May 31, 1975). Houston: Institute for the Arts, Rice University, 1978.

Neuberger, Suzanne, *Rudolf Bauer, 1889–1953.* exhib. cat. Museum Moderner Kunst, Museum des 20 Jahrhundert, Vienna (May 23–July 23, 1985. Vienna: Museum des 20 Jahrhundert, 1985).

Newman, Barnett. *Pre-columbian Stone Sculpture.* exhib. cat. New York, Wakefield Gallery (May 16–June 5, 1944). New York: Wakefield Gallery, 1944.

——. "Escultura precolumbian en piedra." *La Revista Belga,* vol. 1, no. 6 (August 1944): 51–59.

——. *Northwest Coast Indian Painting.* exhib. cat. New York, Betty Parsons Gallery (September 30–October 19, 1946). New York: Betty Parsons Gallery, 1946.

——. *The Ideographic Picture.* exhib. cat. New York, Betty Parsons Gallery (January 20–February 8, 1947). New York: Betty Parsons Gallery, 1947.

——. "The First Man was an Artist." *Tiger's Eye,* vol. 1, no. 1 (October 1947): 57–60.

——. *Sculpture. Ferber.* exhib. cat. New York, Betty Parsons Gallery (December 15, 1947–January 3, 1948). New York: Betty Parsons Gallery, 1948.

——. "The Object and the Image." *Tiger's Eye,* vol. 1, no. 3 (March 1948): 111.

——. "The Ides of Art: Six Opinions on What is Sublime in Art. The Sublime is Now." *Tiger's Eye,* vol. 1, no. 6 (December 1948): 51–53.

——. "The Museum World." *Arts Yearbook,* 9 (1967): 90.

——. Letter to the editor. *Artforum,* vol. 6, no. 7 (March 1968): 4.

——. "For Impassioned Criticism." *Art News,* vol. 67, no. 4 (Summer 1968): 26-27, 58–59.

——. "Chartres and Jericho." *Art News,* vol. 68, no. 2 (April 1969): 29.

O'Doherty, Brian. "Rothko." *Art International,* vol. 14, no. 8 (October 1970): 30–49.

Ortmayer, Roger. "Rothko Newman Chapel." *Kunst und Kirche,* April 1971: 206.

Patton, Phil. "Philip Johnson. The Man Who Changed Houston's Skyline." *Houston City Magazine,* January 1980: 36–46.

Puyo, Jean. "Jean Puyo interroge le Père Congar. Les interviews." *Le Centurion,* 1975.

Rathbone, Eliza. "Mark Rothko: The Brown and Gray Paintings." In *American Art at Mid-Century. The Subjects of the Artist.* exhib. cat. Washington, D.C., National Gallery of Art (June 1, 1978–January 14, 1979). Washington, D.C.: National Gallery of Art, 1978.

Restany, Pierre. "Notes de Voyage: Houston, New York." *Domus,* no. 498 (May 1971): 48–50; reply with rejoinder by D. Buren, *Domus,* no. 502 (September 1971): 56.

Richard, Paul. "A Sculptor Weds Geometry to Wood." *Washington Post,* August 13, 1967: G7: cols. 3–7.

——. "Bladen's X is an X is an X is an X." *Washington Post,* October 8, 1967: K7: cols. 1–4.

——. "Corcoran: People Crisis." *Washington Post,* July 29, 1969: B1: col. 1, B4: col. 1.

——. "Home for the Obelisk." *Washington Post,* August 27, 1969: B13: cols 2–3.

Richardson, Brenda. *Barnett Newman. The Complete Drawings, 1944–1969.* Baltimore: Baltimore Museum of Art, 1979.

Rodman, Selden. *Conversations with Artists.* New York: Devin-Adair, 1957.

Rose, Barbara. "Blowup–The Problem of Scale in Sculpture." *Art in America,* vol. 56, no. 4 (July–August 1968): 80–91.

Rosenberg, Harold. *Barnett Newman: 'Broken Obelisk' and Other Sculptures.* Seattle: University of Washington Press, 1971.

——. *Barnett Newman.* New York: Harry N. Abrams, 1978.

Rosenblum, Robert. *Modern Painting and the Northern Romantic Tradition: Friedrich to Rothko.* New York: Harper and Row, 1975.

Rothko, Mark. [Letter with Adolph Gottlieb to Edward Alden Jewell] In the *New York Times,* June 7, 1943.

——. [Radio broadcast with Adolph Gottlieb] "The Portrait and the Modern Artist." WNYC-FM, October 13, 1943; reprinted in *The New York School. The First Generation. Paintings of the 1940's and 1950's.* exhib. cat. Los Angeles, Los Angeles County Museum (July 16–August 1, 1965): 265; and Irving Sandler, *The Triumph of American Painting. A History of Abstract Expressionism.* New York: Praeger, 1970: 292.

——. "The Romantics Were Prompted." *Possibilities,* no. 1 (Win. 1947/48): 84.

——. [Statement] In *Tiger's Eye,* vol. 1, no. 2 (December 1947): 44; reprinted in *New York School. The First Generation.* Greenwich, CT: New York Graphic Society, 1971: 140.

——. [Statement] In *15 Americans.* exhib. cat. New York, The Museum of Modern Art (March 25–June 11, 1952). New York: The Museum of Modern Art, 1952.

——. [Interview] In Selden Rodman, *Conversations with Artists.* New York: Devin-Adair, 1957. New York: Capricorn Books, 1961: 92–94.

——. [Excerpt] Lecture delivered at Pratt Institute, Brooklyn, 1958; reprinted in *New York School. The First Generation.* Greenwich, CT: New York Graphic Society, 1971: 143.

Rubin, William S. *Modern Sacred Art and the Church of Assy.* New York: Columbia University Press, 1961.

Rudenstine, Angelica. *The Guggenheim Museum Collection: Paintings 1880–1945.* 2 vols. New York: The Solomon R. Guggenheim Museum, 1976.

S'aenz, Kelly Millicent Andrea Gallagher. "The Rothko Chapel: The Slow Arrow of Beauty." M.A. thesis, University of Texas at Austin, 1980.

São Paulo Bienial VII, São Paulo, Brazil. exhib. cat. São Paulo, Brazil (September 4–November 28, 1965); Washington, D.C., National Collection of Fine Arts at the Smithsonian (January 27–March 6, 1966). Pasadena, CA: Pasadena Art Museum [1965]. Essay by Walter Hopps.

Schlumberger, Anne Gruner. *The Schlumberger Adventure.* New York: Arco, 1982.

Schneider, Pierre. "Through the Louvre with Barnett Newman." *Art News,* vol. 68, no. 4 (Summer 1969): 34–40, 70–72.

Sandler, Irving. "Public Art #1," introductory essay to *Sculpture in Environment.* exhib. cat. New York, New York Administration of Recreation and Cultural Affairs for the Cultural Showcase Festival (October 1–31, 1967). New York: Stern Brothers for the Department of Parks, Recreation and Cultural Affairs, 1967.

Seckler, Dorothy Gees. "Frontiers of Space." *Art in America,* vol. 50, no. 2 (Summer 1962): 82–87.

Secrest, Meryle. "A Resignation, An Uproar." *Washington Post,* July 8, 1969: D6: cols. 2–5.

——. "Light is Dimming the National Gallery." *Washington Post,* July 10, 1969: K2: cols. 1–5.

——. "An Era Ends. Corcoran Gallery Obelisk Removed by Creator." *Washington Post,* July 11, 1969: B1: cols. 6–7.

Seitz, William C. *Abstract Expressionist Painting in America.* Cambridge, MA and London, England: Harvard University Press, for the National Gallery of Art, Washington, DC, 1983.

Seldes, Lee. *The Legacy of Mark Rothko.* New York: Holt, Rinehart & Winston, 1978.

Selz, Peter. *Mark Rothko.* exhib. cat. New York, The Museum of Modern Art (Jan. 18–Mar. 12, 1961). New York: The Museum of Modern Art, 1961.

Shirey, David L. "Barney." *Newsweek,* April 14, 1969: 93–94.

Siegel, Jeanne. Review of "Sculpture in Environment." *Arts Magazine,* vol. 42, no. 2 (Nov. 1964): 58.

Singer, Susanna E. *Drawings for Outdoor Sculpture 1946–1977.* exhib. cat. New York, John Weber Gallery (November 1977). New York: John Weber Gallery, 1977.

Slate, Lane, director. [Film interview] *USA Artists: Barnett Newman.* Alan Solomon, writer. New York: National Educational Television, 1966.

Snell, David. "Rothko Chapel–The Painter's Final Testament." *Smithsonian,* August 1971: 46–55.

Solomon, Alan R. *Painting in New York 1944–1969*. exhib. cat. Pasadena, CA, Pasadena Art Museum (November 24, 1969–January 11, 1970). Pasadena, CA: Pasadena Art Museum, 1970.

Solomon R. Guggenheim Foundation. *Art of Tomorrow, Solomon R. Guggenheim Collection of Non-Objective Paintings;* fifth catalogue of the Solomon R. Guggenheim collection, part of which is temporarily exhibited at 14 East 54th Street, New York City. exhib. cat. New York, Solomon R. Guggenheim Foundation (beginning June 1, 1939). New York: Solomon R. Guggenheim Museum, 1939.

Spies, Werner. "Cathedral of Color." *Focus on Art.* New York: Rizzoli, 1982.

Sundell, Nina. *The Robert and Jane Meyerhoff Collection 1958–1979.* [Jane Meyerhoff, 1980].

"Université de Saint Thomas, Houston." *Architecture d'aujourd'hui*, no. 107 (April–May 1963): 26–27.

"USA Artists: Barnett Newman." National Educational Television telecast, WNET-TV, New York, July 12, 1966. Lane Slate, director; Alan Solomon, writer. Copy in Television Archives of the Arts, MoMA.

Waldman, Diane. *Mark Rothko. A Retrospective.* exhib. cat. (traveling 1978–1979). New York: Solomon R. Guggenheim Museum, 1978.

Das zweite Vatikanische Konzil, Konstitutionen, Dekrete, und Erklärungen. 3 vols. Freiberg: Herder, 1966/68.

Unpublished Letters, Documents, Interviews, Verbal Communications

Ambler, Louise. Telephone conversation with Peter Lukehart, November 20, 1986. Notes in Houston, Menil Foundation.

Ashton, Dore. Conversation with Susan Barnes, October 23, 1986. Notes in Houston, Menil Foundation.

Aubry, Eugene. Conversation with John de Menil, April 28, 1972. Notes in Houston, Menil Foundation.

——. Interview with Dominique de Menil and Susan Barnes, January 2, 1979. Notes in Houston, Menil Foundation.

Blinken, Donald M. Letter to Suzannah Doeringer (Fabing), July 3, 1979. Rothko Foundation documentation, National Gallery of Art, Washington, DC.

Corcoran Gallery of Art, Washington, DC. Ledger from Records Group 4: "Exhibition Costs 1960–1967."

——. Ledger from Records Group 4: "Exhibition Income and Expenses, 1968–1971."

——. Ledger with "Gifts and Favors from Members and Non-Members, 1964–1970."

Cousins, Judith. Conversation with Peter Lukehart, November 26, 1986. Notes in Houston, Menil Foundation.

di Suvero, Mark. Letter to Eleanor (Sue) Green, n.d. [1967]. Archives of American Art, Washington, D.C. (uncatalogued).

Doeringer, Suzannah (Fabing). Letter to Donald M. Blinken, July 10, 1979. Rothko Foundation documentation, National Gallery of Art, Washington, DC.

Edwards, Roy. Interview with Stephany Crosby, April 1977. Tape and transcript in Houston, Menil Foundation.

Fabing, Suzannah. Interview with Susan Barnes, October 28, 1986. Notes in Houston, Menil Foundation.

Farenthold, Frances Tarlton. Letter to John and Dominique de Menil, August 26, 1969. Menil Foundation.

Ferber, Herbert. Interview with Dominique de Menil and Susan Barnes, September 6, 1981. Tape and transcript in Houston, Menil Foundation.

Fralin, Frances. Conversation with Peter Lukehart, October 21, 1986. Notes in Houston, Menil Foundation.

Geldzahler, Henry. Telephone conversation with Peter Lukehart, January 1987. Notes in Houston, Menil Foundation.

Glimcher, Arnold. Interview with Dominique de Menil, February 8, 1979. Tape and transcript in Houston, Menil Foundation.

Green, Eleanor. Interview with Susan Barnes and Peter Lukehart, October 3, 1986. Notes in Houston, Menil Foundation.

——. Interview with Peter Lukehart, October 22, 1986. Notes in Houston, Menil Foundation.

Green, Wilder. Conversation with Susan Barnes, November 21, 1986. Notes in Houston, Menil Foundation.

Hines, John E. Letter to John de Menil, August 26, 1969. Menil Foundation.

Houston Municipal Arts Commission. Memorandum from the Municipal Arts Commission, May 27, 1969. Menil Foundation.

Jensen, Deborah. Conversation with Peter Lukehart, November 24, 1986. Notes in Houston, Menil Foundation.

Johnson, Philip. Interview with Dominique de Menil and Susan Barnes, winter 1979. Tape and transcript in Houston, Menil Foundation.

——. Interview with Susan Barnes, June 15, 1982. Tape in Houston, Menil Foundation.

Kelly, Ray. Interview with Carol Mancusi-Ungaro and Mary Jane Victor, May 30, 1980. Tape and transcript in Houston, Menil Foundation.

——. Conversation with Susan Barnes, August 23, 1983. Notes in Houston, Menil Foundation.

Kuh, Katharine. Interview with Dominique de Menil and Susan Barnes, March 13, 1981. Tape and transcript in Houston, Menil Foundation.

Legg, Alicia. Conversation with Peter Lukehart, November 25, 1986. Notes in Houston, Menil Foundation.

Lippincott, Donald. Interview with Peter Lukehart, October 22, 1986. Notes in Houston, Menil Foundation.

——. Interview with Peter Lukehart, November 20, 1986. Notes in Houston, Menil Foundation.

——. Telephone conversation with Peter Lukehart, January 15, 1987. Notes in Houston, Menil Foundation.

Little, Nancy. Letter to Peter Lukehart, November 18, 1986. Menil Foundation.

Little, Nancy. Conversation with Peter Lukehart, December 8, 1986. Notes in Houston, Menil Foundation.

MacAgy, Douglas. Letter to Mrs. Newton Wray, June 24, 1969.
Menil Foundation.

——. Letter to John de Menil, July 28, 1969. Menil Foundation.

Marcus, Stanley. Letter to John and Dominique de Menil, August 28, 1969. Menil Foundation.

Menil, Dominique de. Conversation with Susan Barnes, December 30, 1978. Notes in Houston, Menil Foundation.

——. Conversation with Susan Barnes, September 6, 1981. Notes in Houston, Menil Foundation.

Menil, John de. Letter to Mrs. Newton Wray, June 30, 1969. Menil Foundation.

——. Letter to Douglas MacAgy, July 21, 1969. Menil Foundation.

——. Letter to Douglas MacAgy, August 2, 1969. Menil Foundation.

——. Letter to Douglas MacAgy, August 12, 1969. Menil Foundation.

Morris, Martha. Conversation with Peter Lukehart, October 21, 1986. Notes in Houston, Menil Foundation.

Motherwell, Robert. Interview with Dominique de Menil and Susan Barnes, May 10, 1980. Tape and transcript in Houston, Menil Foundation.

Murray, Robert. Interview with Peter Lukehart, November 20, 1986. Notes in Houston, Menil Foundation.

——. Interview with Peter Lukehart, December 2, 1986. Notes in Houston, Menil Foundation.

Newman, Annalee. Conversation with Susan Barnes, October 18, 1986. Notes in Houston, Menil Foundation.

Newman, Barnett. Letter to Herman Warner Williams, November 7, 1967. Archives of American Art, MF 3567, Eleanor Broome Green letters, 205–216.

——. Letter to John de Menil, June 8, 1969. Menil Foundation.

——. Letter to John and Dominique de Menil, August 26, 1969. Menil Foundation.

Olivier, Katherine. Conversation with Peter Lukehart, November 20, 1986. Notes in Houston, Menil Foundation.

Reinhardt Bedford, Rita. Interview with Dominique de Menil and Susan Barnes, September 13, 1980. Tape and transcript in Houston, Menil Foundation.

Richard, Paul. Conversation with Peter Lukehart, October 1986.

Scharf, William. Interview with Carol Mancusi-Ungaro and Mary Jane Victor, June 1, 1980. Tape and transcript in Houston, Menil Foundation.

——. Interview with Susan Barnes, June 24, 1982. Tape in Houston, Menil Foundation.

Schwabacher, Ethel. Conversation with Susan Barnes, July 1981. Notes in Houston, Menil Foundation.

Seckler, Edward. Conversation with Peter Lukehart, October 30, 1986. Notes in Houston, Menil Foundation.

Selz, Peter. Conversation with Susan Barnes, November 22, 1986. Notes in Houston, Menil Foundation.

Shannon, Thompson. Interview with Susan Barnes, June 29, 1982. Tape in Houston, Menil Foundation.

Smith, Arthur Hall. Conversation with Susan Barnes, January 12, 1987. Notes in Houston, Menil Foundation.

Tsirantonakis, Margaret. Conversation with Peter Lukehart, November 24, 1986.

Widrig, Walter and Philip Oliver-Smith. Conversation with Susan Barnes, February 7, 1982. Notes in Houston, Menil Foundation.

Williams, Alice (Mrs. Herman Warner). Conversation with Peter Lukehart, November 21, 1986.

Winkler, Helen. Interview with Susan Barnes, June 27, 1982. Tape in Houston, Menil Foundation.

Winkler, Paul. Conversation with Susan Barnes, October 21, 1986. Notes in Houston, Menil Foundation.

Withers Swan Agency (New York). "Martin Luther King Honored in Houston: The Man and His Work Commemorated in Monumental Sculpture," press release, August 8, 1969. Menil Foundation.

Wray, Katherine (Mrs. Newton). Letter to John de Menil, June 10, 1969. Menil Foundation.

Rothko Chapel Events

1971

Dedication of the Rothko Chapel, *February 27*

Dedication of the *Broken Obelisk, February 28*

Musical service by the Symphony of Souls in Christ from the Cathedral of St. John the Divine, New York, *June 22*

Poetry reading by Stanley Kunitz, a friend of Mark Rothko, *November 7*

United Presbyterian Church Sunday School senior class, *November 14*

A program of hymns with guitar accompaniment by a group of thirty seminarians from St. Mary's Seminary, *December 3*

Muslim prayers, Islamic Society of Greater Houston, *every Sunday*

Eucharistic Liturgy, University of St. Thomas, *every Thursday*

1972

The first ecumenical service observing Martin Luther King's birthday, *January 15*

Catholic–Protestant Vesper Service in observance of the Universal Week of Prayer for Christian Unity, *January 22*

Eid el-Adha prayers, Muslim Feast, Islamic Society of Greater Houston, *January 27*

Fairhaven Methodist Church Youth Ministry: young people playing electronic music, *February 13*

Machaut Mass with medieval instruments, Music Department, University of St. Thomas, *February 28*

A film of an interview with an inmate soon to be released from State prison and an official of the New Directions program of the University of Texas School of Public Health, *March 13*

St. Luke's Methodist Youth Ministry, *March 26*

Premiere of Morton Feldman's "The Rothko Chapel," conducted by Maurice Peress of the Corpus Christi

Symphony, with forty-eight members of the Houston Symphony Chorale conducted by Donald Strong, *April 9*

Ecumenical Liturgy "Festival of Life," University of St. Thomas Chaplains, *August 26*

Convocation ceremony, Institute of Religion and Human Development, *September 8*

Day of Atonement observance, National Conference of Christians and Jews, led by Sr. Ann Gillen, S.S.I., *September 17*

Ecumenical service every first Wednesday of each month, starting October 4, led by the Reverend John Minter, Montrose Ministry.

Eid el-Fitr prayers, Islamic Society of Greater Houston, *November 7*

Early Christmas celebration, Montrose Ministry, *December 6*

1973

Zazen Buddhist Meditation Group, *every Tuesday and Thursday in January*

Traditional Modes of Contemplation and Action in World Religions, *(Colloquium I):* (left to right), *Yusuf Ibish, Allahbuksh K. Brohi, Joseph Epes Brown, Leo Schaya, Wande Abimbola and Victor Danner, 1973*

Ruhani Satsang Meditation Group, led by Joe Wardwell, *every first and third Sunday afternoon in January*

Eid el-Adha prayers, Islamic Society of Greater Houston, *January 15*

Ralph Kirkpatrick: Harpsichord recital of J. S. Bach's "Goldberg Variations," *February 11*

World Day of Prayer Service, sponsored by Church Women United, *March 2*

Christian Worship on the first day of Lent, Montrose Ministry, *March 9*

St. Luke's Methodist Youth Ministry, *March 20*

Convocation Ceremony by the Institute of Religion and Human Development, *March 24*

Anniversary of Martin Luther King's assassination observed by the Black Students' Union, University of St. Thomas, *April 4*

A pre-Palm Sunday Celebration by the Montrose Ministry, *April 11*

A service in celebration of the city: "Reflections for Easter," *April 11*

Liturgical service by the graduate program in Religious Education, University of St. Thomas, *Thursday afternoon: June 14, 21 and 28, July 5, 12, and 19*

Colloquium I: "Traditional Modes of Contemplation and Action," *July 22–30*

Organized by Yusuf Ibish, American University of Beirut

Participants: Wande Abimbola, Shojun Bando, A. K. Brohi, Esq., Joseph Epes Brown, Victor Danner, Yusuf Ibish, Toshihiko Izutsu, Archbishop Georges Khodr, Lama Lobsang P. Lhalungpa, T.M.P. Mahadevan, Seyyed Hossein Nasr, Jacob Needleman, Raimundo Panikkar, Awadh Kishore Saran, Leo Schaya, André Scrima, Huston Smith, al-Sayyedah Fatimah al-Yashrutiyya, Elémire Zolla.

Musicians: Jihad Abu-Mrad, Munir Bashir, Pandit Pran Nath, Daryush Safvat, Nur al-Din Sarvistani.

Orientation Week Service by the University of St. Thomas, *August*

Rosh Hashanah observance, *September 27*

Christian Day of Atonement—Yom Kippur, National Conference of Christians and Jews, *October 5*

Puja, Hindu Worship Society, *October 14*

Eid el-Fitr prayers, Islamic Society, *October 28*

Roberto Rossellini, Colloquium II – Human Rights / Human Reality, 1973

Steve Reich Concert, *November 11*

Colloquium II: "Human Rights/Human Reality," *December 8–9*

Organized by: Roberto Rossellini and Simone Swan

Participants: John Calhoun, Dom Helder Camara, Joel Elkes, Giorgio La Pira, former mayor of Florence, Jonas Salk.

1974

Eid el-Adha prayers, The Islamic Society, *January 4*

Puja, Hindu Worship Society, *January 13*

Poetry reading by Kenward Elmslie and John Ashbery, *March 6*

Christian Lenten Service, The Reverend John Minter, *March 21*

Anniversary of Martin Luther King's assassination observed by the Black Students' Union, University of St. Thomas, *April 4*

Puja, Hindu Worship Society, *August 10*

Orientation Liturgy for students, University of St. Thomas, *August 25*

Christian Day of Atonement/Yom Kippur, *September 25*

Puja, Hindu Worship Society, *October 13*

Eid el-Fitr prayers, The Islamic Society, *October 17*

A gathering of young people interested in furthering the aims of the Taize Monastery Council with Mildred de Broucker, *November 22–24*

Community Advent Celebration, The Reverend John Minter, *December 12*

University of St. Thomas Graduation Mass, *December 20*

Eid el-Adha prayers, The Islamic Society, *December 24*

Broadcast of Colloquium II on PBS, *December 28, 29*

1975

Juan Capra: Recital, *February 16*

Karlheinz Stockhausen: "Hymnen," *March 2*

Palm Sunday Mass, University of St. Thomas, *March 23*

Peace Celebration by Quakers, *May 17*

Christian Day of Atonement/Yom Kippur, National Conference of Christians and Jews, *September 15*

Jain Service by Muni Shushil Kumar, *September 21*

Eid el-Fitr prayers, The Islamic Society, *October 6*

Inter-denominational Advent service, University of St. Thomas, *in December*

1976

Martin Luther King's birthday observance: an ecumenical service, *January 15*

Palm Sunday Mass, *April 11*

Pro Musicis Foundation recital, *April 11*

Prayers for Peace (Lebanon, South Africa, Ireland), *June 6*

Diane Tobola & Wolfgang Justen, Recital, *September 28*

An evening of Baroque Chamber Music, University of St. Thomas, *November 16*

Eid al-Adha prayers, The Islamic Society, *December 2*

Human Rights Day Observance: a program of recorded music from different musical traditions selected by ethnomusicologist Alan Lomax, and the reading of the thirty articles of the United Nations Declaration of Human Rights by Houstonians of thirteen different countries representing thirteen different religions, *December 9*

1977

Martin Luther King's birthday observance: an interfaith service, *January 16*

Colloquium III: "Toward a New Strategy for Development", *February 3–5*

Organized by James W. Land, Rice University, Houston

Participants: Harold Brookfield, Fernando Enrique Cardoso, Richard Cooper, Reginald Green, Albert O. Hirschman, Nurul Islam, Bagicha Singh Minhas, Goran Ohlin, Dudley Seers, Paul Streeten, Bill Warren.

Evening of prayer and song, "Foundation of Faith," *May 4*

Charismatic Mass, *October 16*

I–We–You Interfaith Worship Experience: Women in Religion, *November 20*

Human Rights Day observance: Houston Independent School District and the Houston chapter of the United Nations sponsored poster contest expressing ideas of freedom, *December 11*

Mid-term Mass, University of St. Thomas, *December 21*

1978

Martin Luther King's birthday observance: an interfaith service, *January 15*

"A Time for Prayer," prayers offered by Muslims, U.C.C. (Congregationalists), Copts, Jews, Quakers, Episcopalians, Catholics, Greek Orthodox, Lutherans, *January 8, 15, 22, 29, February 5, 12, 19, 26, March 5*

Wheat Shipment to Vietnam celebration: Church World Service, Texas Conference of Churches, Houston Metropolitan Ministries, and Church Women United held an ecumenical service to mark the culmination of a national campaign to sail a ship of wheat to Vietnam as an expression of postwar reconciliation, *March 4*

Good Friday commemoration, *March 24*

The Whirling Dervishes: six "Sema" celebrations by the Mevlevi Dervishes from Konya, Turkey, *October 15–22*

Human Rights Day observance: "International Year of the Child" was initiated by students from the Guadalupe School for Undocumented Children. Eighty-five youngsters prayed, sang, and shared their thoughts in English and Spanish, *December 10*

"Redemption in Every Age: Passover Freedom Service,"
Rabbi L. Hoffman and Cantor W. Sharlin, 1981

1979

Martin Luther King's birthday observance: film: "From Montgomery to Memphis," *January 15*

Palm Sunday Mass, University of St. Thomas, *April 8*

His Holiness the Dalai Lama's visit and meeting with scientists and religious leaders, *September 18–19*

Participants: Dom Helder Camara, Joel Elkes, M.D., Rabbi Arthur Hertzberg, Professor Yusuf Ibish, The Reverend James Lawson, William S. Merwin, The Reverend Francis X. Murphy, Octavio Paz, Professor Paul Schimmel, Professor André Scrima, Professor Jane I. Smith, Professor Frederick J. Streng, and Professor Robert A.F. Thurman.

Interfaith gathering dedicated to end hunger, *September 22*

Universal Worship, an ecumenical service, *November 11*

Human Rights Day observance: "Thinking Globally, Acting Locally," speaker Leonel Castillo, Commissioner—U.S. Immigration & Naturalization Ser., *December 9*

Music marking the holy days: Hannukah music, *December 16*; Christmas music, *December 23*; New Age Music for the new year, *December 30*

1980

Martin Luther King's birthday observance. Speaker: The Reverend Joseph E. Lowery, President of Southern Christian Leadership Conference, *January 16*

The Royal Dancers and Musicians of Bhutan, co-sponsored with the Asia Society/Houston, *April 9*

Celebration of *Dhikr* "Remembrance of God," with Sheikh Muzaffar Ozak and the Halveti-Jerrahi Dervishes of Istanbul, *April 13*

Hassidic Music and Workshop, Rabbi Schlomo Carlebach and Rabbi Samuel A. Karff, *April 26–27*

Universal Worship, an interfaith service for world peace, *June 8*

St. Romano's Chorale, Music from the Eastern Orthodox Tradition, *July 19*

World Peace Day, Baha'i prayers in sixteen languages, *September 21*

Expression of the Spirit—Music and Architecture; this program was part of a Conference on the Arts and Religious Communities in Houston, *October 8*

Annual Service Award by National Conference of Christians and Jews, *November 23*

Human Rights Day observance: "Human Rights and the General Welfare," speaker: Bob Eckhardt, Congressman, *December 14*

1981

Martin Luther King's birthday observance: "Towards Justice," speaker: Ronald V. Dellums, Congressman, *January 15*

Redemption in Every Age: A Passover Celebration; a service designed by Rabbi Lawrence A. Hoffman, *April 21*

The First Rothko Chapel Awards for Commitment to Truth and Freedom, *June 20*

Recipients: Giuseppe Alberigo, Italy; Amadou Hampaté Bâ, Mali; Balys Gajauskas, U.S.S.R.; Douglas and Joan Grant, California; Las Madres de la Plaza de Mayo, Argentina; Ned O'Gorman, New York; Warren Robbins, Washington, D.C.; Sakokwenonkwas (Chief Tom Porter), The Mohawk Nation at Akwesasne, Raquette Point, NY; Zwelakhe Sisulu, South Africa; Socorro Juridico and Roberto Cuellar, El Salvador; Tatiana Velikanova, U.S.S.R.; Jose Zalaquett, Chile.

Colloquium IV: "Islam: Spiritual Message and Quest for Justice," *October 21–25*

Organized by Nadjm ud-Din Bammat, Delegate of the Org. of the Islamic Conference to UNESCO, Paris.

Participants: Ms. Etel Adnan, Khurshid Ahmad, Syed Muhammed Naguib al-Attas, Hamid Algar, Muazzam

Ali, al-Sadig al-Mahdi, Prince Muhammad al-Faisal al-Saud, Salem Azzam, Nadjm ud-Din Bammat, Ahmad Ben Bella, Ms. Sahair el-Calamawy, Hisham Djait, Ms. Emel Esin, Ahmad Fouatih, Yusuf Ibish, Javid Iqbal, Ali Kettani, Muhsen Mahdi, Hisham Nashabeh, Abdus Salam, Mohammad Talbi, Ms. Eva de Vitray Meyerovitch.

Pandit Pran Nath *Morning Ragas, November 15*

Steve Reich, American premiere of *Tehillim, November 21–22*

Human Rights Day observance: "Struggle for Human Rights in the Soviet Union," speaker: Dr. Cronid Lubarsky, exiled Soviet scientist and human rights advocate; Editor of U.S.S.R. News Brief, *December 10*

1982

Martin Luther King's birthday observance: "A Man for This Season," a panel discussion with: Fred Baldwin, Rabbi Moshe Cahana, Lex Hixon, Professor Nathan Irvin Huggins, The Reverend William Lawson, Congressman Mickey Leland, and Judge Gabrielle K. McDonald, *January 15*

Prayers for a peaceful world, Baha'i service, *March 21*

Palm Sunday and Good Friday services, University of St. Thomas, *April 4, 9*

A Weekend of Worship and Witness for Pentecost, Peace Sabbath, and Memorial Day, *May 28–31*

Hiroshima—Nagasaki Commemoration around the *Broken Obelisk, August 6*

Annual Service Award by National Conference of Christians and Jews, *November 22*

Human Rights Day observance: "Human Rights in Africa," speaker: Ambassador James Victor Gbeho, Ambassador from Ghana to the United Nations, U.N. Special Committee Against Apartheid, *December 10*

1983

Martin Luther King's birthday observance: "International Human Rights in Central America and the Role of the Church in Liberation Movements," speaker: Robert F. Drinan, S. J., *January 16*

Palm Sunday and Good Friday services, University of St. Thomas, *March 27, April 1*

"Nuclear Arms Policy and Disarmament" by Dr. Jerome B. Wiesner, President Emeritus, M.I.T., at the Chapel House, *April 5*

Pandit Pran Nath: *Morning Ragas, April 17*

Peace Vigil organized by Jane Abell, O. P., *May 21*

Baha'i Service, *June 11*

Celebration of *Dhikr* "Remembrance of God," with Sheikh Muzaffar Ozak, the Halveti-Jerrahi Dervishes and the Musicians of Istanbul, *October 4, 6*

Colloquium V: "Ethnicities and Nations: Processes of Inter-Ethnic Relations in Latin America, Southeast Asia, and The Pacific, *October 28–30*

Organized by: Francesco Pellizzi, Peabody Museum, Harvard University; Stanley J. Tambiah, Harvard University; Remo Guidieri, University of Paris X, Nanterre.

Participants: Benedict Anderson, Alain Babadzan, Alicia M. Barabas, Miguel A. Bartolomé, Guillermo Bonfil, Jorge Bustamente, Georges Condominas, Gemma Cruz, William Cunningham, Roxanne Dunbar Ortiz, Michael Fischer, Remo Guidieri, Carlos Guzman, Cornelia Ann Kammerer, Burhan Magenda, Cesar Adib Majul, Margarita Melville, Jacques Népote, Francesco Pellizzi, Surin Pitsuwan, Rodolfo Stavenhagen, Stanley J. Tambiah, Serge Thion, Stefano Varese.

The 35th Anniversary of the Universal Declaration of Human Rights was marked by signing petitions in an International Campaign for a Universal Amnesty for Prisoners of Conscience (initiated by Andrei Sakharov and inaugurated by Amnesty International, December 10th, 1982) *December 10*

Zoroastrian New Year Rites, 1986.

1984

Martin Luther King's birthday observance: Houston premiere of "The March" by filmmaker James Blue, and the Texas Southern University Choir, *January 15*

"South Africa Today: Critical Issues, Critical Choices," speaker: Donald Woods, exiled South African journalist and news editor, author of banned work about Steve Biko, *March 8*

Palm Sunday and Good Friday services, University of St. Thomas, *April 15, 20*

Concert of Sephardic music to celebrate the Jewish Holy Days by *Alhambra,* a musical group led by Isabelle Ganz, *September 23*

Human Rights Day observance: speaker: President Jimmy Carter, *December 10*

1985

Martin Luther King's birthday observance: The Boys Choir of Harlem, *January 13*

Celebration of the Vernal Equinox New Year by the Houston Zoroastrian community, *March 21*

Tibetan Buddhist rituals presented by the Gyuto Tantric Monks of Tibet under the patronage of His Holiness the Dalai Lama, *April 16–17*

Prayer for peace in Vietnam by the Vietnamese Association of Houston, *April 27*

Zoroastrian rites, *August 23*

Rosh Hashanah observance, *September 15*

Yom Kippur Service, *September 24*

Annual Service Award by National Conference of Christians and Jews, *November 24*

Houston Interfaith Thanksgiving Service (Jews, Christians, and Muslims), *November 26*

Human Rights Day observance: "The Absence of Human Rights," speaker: Nthato Motlana, a prominent physician and chairman of the Citizens' Association of Soweto, *December 10*

1986

Zoroastrian new year rites, *March 21*

Palm Sunday and Good Friday services, University of St. Thomas, *March 23, 28*

"Meditations" by New Music America, *April 5*

Mass following Second Oscar Romero Award ceremony, 1988, (left to right) Rosalynn Carter, Dominique de Menil and Paulo Evaristo Cardinal Arns

"Miracles" by the Folger Consort, *April 20*

Annual Service Award by National Conference of Christians and Jews, *November 23*

Houston Interfaith Thanksgiving Service (Jews, Christians, and Muslims), *November 25*

The Second Rothko Chapel Awards for Commitment to Truth and Freedom, and the **Carter-Menil Human Rights Prize,** *December 10*

Keynote Address: The Most Reverend Desmond M. Tutu, Archbishop of Capetown

Recipients of Rothko Chapel Awards: Charter 77, Czechoslovakia; Myles Horton, U.S.A.; Helen Joseph and Albertina Sisulu, South Africa; Anatoly Koryagin, U.S.S.R.; Jonathan Kuttab and Raja Shehadeh, Occupied West Bank; Sanctuary, U.S.A.

The First Oscar Romero Award:

Recipient: Bishop Leonidas Proaño Villalba, Ecuador

The Carter-Menil Human Rights Prize:

Recipients: Grupo de Apoyo Mutuo (The Group for Mutual Support), Guatemala; Yuri Orlov, U.S.S.R.

1987

Zoroastrian new year rites, *March 21*

Vigil for the Commemoration of Archbishop Oscar Romero's death, *March 26*

Palm Sunday and Good Friday services, University of St. Thomas, *April 12, 17*

Ecumenical service for the "Caravan of the Forgotten," *May 16*

World premiere: "Mass for Pentecost Sunday (in memory of Russ)," by Richard Landry, commissioned for The Menil Collection opening, *June 4, 5, 7*

Zoroastrian rites, *August 25*

Mass with gregorian singing; Kantores chorale conducted by Don Bonifacio, Baroffio Abbey, S. Maria della Scala in Nochi, Bari, Italy (in conjunction with *Italy in Houston* Festival), *October 18*

Ecumenical Service "Peace on Earth Begins at Home" (against violence at home), *October 25*

Houston Interfaith Thanksgiving Service (Jews, Christians, and Muslims), *November 23*

Buddhist service, *December 9*

1988

Ash Wednesday Service, ecumenical community observance, the Covenant Baptist Church, *February 17*

The Second Oscar Romero Award, *March 24*

Recipient: Paulo Evaristo Cardinal Arns, São Paulo, Brazil

Speakers: Cyrus Vance, Rosalynn Carter, Donald B. Easum

A mass in the park was concelebrated by Cardinal Arns and Bishop Enrique San Pedro immediately following the Award ceremony.

Palm Sunday Mass, University of St. Thomas, *March 27*

Seminar on the Religions of Asia; an event co-sponsored with the Asia Society/Houston, *April 9–10*

Speakers: Ainslee T. Embree, John Esposito, Donald K. Swearer, Tu Wei-ming, Paul Varley.

Interfaith service by the Houston Metropolitan Ministries to install their new Executive Director, *May 19*

"Taking Liberties, The Current Rise of Censorship in America": marathon readings from books currently being banned in communities and schools across the United States, presented by Southwest PEN and The Live Oak Foundation, *June 23*

"Perceptions of Human Rights Issues by Young Americans", a one-day workshop where students from six universities presented papers on a variety of topics to a concerned audience, *October 15*

As a result of this program, two college students and two high school students were chosen to attend in Paris, France an international human rights conference sponsored by the Special Committee of International Non-Governmental Organizations on Human Rights of the United Nations (Geneva) and France Libertés–Fondation Danielle Mitterand (Paris). *December 8–10*

Houston Interfaith Thanksgiving Service, (Jews, Christians, Muslims) *November 22*

The Rothko Chapel extends its hospitality for personal ceremonial events such as baptisms, bar mitzvahs, weddings, and memorial services.

Rothko Chapel Publications:

Contemplation and Action in World Religions, editors, Y. Ibish and I. Marculescu. Distributed by University of Washington Press, Seattle and London, 1978 (abridged paperback version of Colloquium I).

Toward a New Strategy for Development, editors, James W. Land and Kim Q. Hill. Distributed by Pergamon Press, Inc., New York, Oxford, Toronto, Paris, Frankfurt, Sydney, 1979 (all papers presented at Colloquium III).

Ethnicities and Nations: Processes of Interethnic Relations in Latin America, Southeast Asia, and the Pacific, editors, Remo Guidieri, Francesco Pellizzi, Stanley J. Tambiah. Distributed by University of Texas Press, Austin, 1988 (papers presented at Colloquium V).

Dom Helder Camara, Colloquium II – Human Rights/ Human Reality, 1973

Acknowledgements

As a native Houstonian, I am keenly aware of the change that the Rothko Chapel has made in the cultural and spiritual climate of the city. While living in Houston, I was an excited observer of the installation and early years of the chapel. I did not, however, have the good fortune to know Mark Rothko.

This account could not have been written without the generous help of many people who were Rothko's friends and collaborators. Dore Ashton, Eugene Aubry, Howard Barnstone, Roy Edwards, Herbert Ferber, Wilder Green, Philip Johnson, Ray Kelly, Katharine Kuh, Robert Motherwell, Rita Reinhardt, William Scharf, Peter Selz, Helen Winkler, and Rothko's daughter Kate Prizel, shared their memories of Rothko in interviews with Dominique de Menil, myself, or with Menil Collection staff members. They provided essential information on Rothko: his beliefs, his attitudes, his intentions, and his working methods. To them go my deepest thanks, and the thanks of all who care about Rothko's life and work.

I am particularly indebted to the research of Mary Jane Victor and to the following staff members of The Menil Collection: Carol Mancusi-Ungaro, Conservator; Neil Printz, Research Curator; Susan Davidson, Assistant Curator; Harris Rosenstein, Editorial Counsel; John Kaiser, Editorial Associate; Deborah Jensen, Research Associate; and Gayle de Gregori. Special gratitude goes to Bonnie Clearwater and Dana Cranmer of the Mark Rothko Foundation, who responded cheerfully to successive rounds of questions and requests, and who shared many insights. Recollections about Barnett Newman's *Broken Obelisk* were kindly provided by Annalee Newman, Eleanor Green, Don Lippincott and Robert Murray.

While in the throes of writing one carries one's concerns about, and often profits greatly from the ideas of a variety of sensitive listeners. In this category I would like to thank Claude Cernuschi, Isabella Ducrot, Molly Kelly, Elisabeth Kieven, Mina Marefat, Beatrice Mosca, Jim and Kathy Muehlemann, Eliza Rathbone, Ethel Schwabacher, Suzanne Stratton, Walter Widrig, and Paul Winkler. Bertrand Davezac, Katharine Kuh, Herbert Ferber, Walter Hopps, Patricia Toomey, and William Scharf kindly read the typescript and offered their suggestions. The penultimate draft of this text was written during my tenure as a David E. Finley Fellow at the Center for Advanced Study in the Visual Arts, National Gallery of Art, whose support I gratefully acknowledge. In the final stages, Peter Lukehart's energy, thoroughness, and discernment in assistance on research, particularly for Newman's *Broken Obelisk,* and his editorial suggestions were invaluable.

First and last I tender thanks to Dominique de Menil and her late husband John, whose act of faith gave us the Rothko Chapel. To them, and to the memory of Howard Barnstone, this study is lovingly dedicated.

Susan J. Barnes
June, 1987

Design:
Don Quaintance – Public Address Design, Houston

Printing, halftones and separations:
Gardner Lithograph, Los Angeles

Binding:
Roswell Bookbinders, Phoenix

Typesetting:
TEXSource, Houston – composed in ITC Galliard
Arvin C. Conrad, TEX Consultant

Photography Credits:
Figure numbers are listed; except where italics indicate page location of unnumbered illustrations

Hélène Adant, Paris   5
Eve Arnold, London   19, 20
From– Barnstone and Aubry, Houston   42, 59, 60
From– The Bettmann Archive, Inc., New York   68
Charles Bueb, Paris   13
Henri Cartier-Bresson, Paris   11, 58
Geoffrey Clements, New York   4
Father Courier, O.P., Paris   8
David Crossley, Houston   81; *118, 119, 124*
From– Edizione Ardo de Luxe, Venice   43, 44
Rick Gardner, Houston   57
From– The Harvard University, Cambridge   17, 18
Lucien Hervé, Paris   10, 12
Paul Hester, Houston   25, 27, 28, 33, 40, 65; *18*
Hickey & Robertson, Houston   frontispiece; plates I, II, III, IV;
    3, 45, 61, 62, 63, 66, 70, 71, 72, 73, 75, 76, 77, 79; *100*
Max Hirschfield, Washington, D.C.   15
From– The Houston Chronicle   78
From– Howard Barnstone Collection, Houston Public Library,
    Houston Metropolitan Research Center   47, 58
Consuelo Kanaga, New York   *20*
Paul Katz, New York   64
Jim Lemoine, Houston   *122*
Alexander Liberman, New York   cover, 29, 32; *10, 14*
From– The Mark Rothko Foundation, New York   30, 31, 34, 35,
    36, 37, 38, 39
Merlin, Assy   9
From– The Metropolitan Museum of Art, New York   67
Frank Lotz Miller, New Orleans   24
From – The Museum of Modern Art, New York   16
Hans Namuth, New York   23
From– The National Gallery of Art, Washington, D.C.   2
Roger Powers, The Houston Post   74
From– Harold Rosenberg, *Barnett Newman*   69
From– Rothko Chapel, Houston   80, 82, 83; *16, 121, 123*
Warren Skaaren, Houston   7
Fred Stein, New York   21
Ezra Stoller, New York   22
From– The Tate Gallery, London   6, 14
From– Walker Art Center, Minneapolis   1
Janet Woodard, Houston   26, 46, 48, 49, 50, 51, 52, 53, 54, 55, 56

The Rothko Chapel was incorporated in the State of Texas on October 3, 1972. The incorporators were Reuben W. Askanase, John de Menil, Roberto Rossellini and Thompson L. Shannon.

Friends and supporters raised over $150,000. The original donors were Reuben and Hilda Askanase, Eric and Sylvie Boissonnas, André Crispin, Nina Cullinan, Henri Doll, Miles Glaser, Anne Gruner Schlumberger, The Hobby Foundation, Ruth Carter Johnson, Theodore and Caroline Law, Stanley Marcus, Genevieve Peterkin, Floranz Pew, Fayez Sarofim, The Scurlock Foundation and others.

Rothko Chapel   1409 Sul Ross   Houston, Texas 77006
Tel: (713) 524-9839